WHERE ARE YOU REALLY FROM?

 ## ADAM RUTHERFORD

WITH E.L. NORRY   **ILLUSTRATED BY ADAM MING**

CONTENTS

C29 0000 0934 891

'Laugh out loud funny – and you'll learn lots too!'
Adam Kay, author of *Kay's Anatomy*

'A BRILLIANT book about biology and belonging. Packed
to its covers with fascinating facts, science and joy;I have a ten
year old son who will LOVE this book.'
Dr Alice Roberts, author of *The Incredible Human Journey*

'Funny, silly and utterly rigorous – a book that will inspire awe
and wonder in all that read it. It stands a better chance of making
the world a better place than any book I've read recently.'
Dr Chris van Tullekan, author of *Operation Ouch* series

'Only Adam can make the serious business of evolution this much fun.'
**Dr Hannah Fry, author of *Rutherford and Fry's Complete Guide
to Absolutely Everything***

'A fascinating and funny guide to who we are and how we got here.'
Katya Balen, author of *October, October*

'As funny as it's informative - every school
library should have a copy. I learned as I lolled.'
Anthony McGowan, author of *Lark*

FOR JUNO

WITH SPECIAL THANKS TO E. L. NORRY

First published in Great Britain in 2023 by Wren & Rook

Text copyright © Adam Rutherford 2023

Illustrations copyright © Adam Ming 2023

ISBN: 978 1 5263 6424 1

3 5 7 9 10 8 6 4 2

MIX
Paper from
responsible sources
FSC® C104740

Wren & Rook
An imprint of
Hachette Children's Group
Part of Hodder & Stoughton
Carmelite House
50 Victoria Embankment
London EC4Y 0DZ
An Hachette UK Company

www.hachette.co.uk
www.hachettechildrens.co.uk

Printed in Poland

INTRODUCTION

WHO DO YOU
THINK YOU ARE?

Have you ever wondered if you are secretly related to someone **FAMOUS**? A person who is much more exciting and interesting than your annoying sister, your smelly brother or your Great Uncle Roger who you've never met but lives in Spain and sends you a card with £5 in it every birthday (despite the concept of inflation making £5 less valuable each birthday)? Well, wonder no more, because I'm about to let you in on a secret – one that will blow your mind. Ready? OK, alongside your close family – parents, brothers and sisters, Great Uncle Roger – you are definitely also descended from **vicious Vikings, extraordinary emperors, pharaohs of Egypt, great queens or useless kings**!

Yes, you read that right, Your Majesty. **You are absolutely, truly, 100% descended from royalty.** Which makes you pretty special. In fact, everyone is. I'm here to tell you how, and why.

Over the next few pages, we are going to go on an extraordinary adventure through millions of years of human history. We're going to go right the way back to the beginning of humankind and then keep going back to the beginning of life on Earth, and even the birth of the Earth itself. We're going to meet all sorts of creatures who are your ancestors, from wormy things in the ancient oceans all the way to hairy apes and less hairy kings and queens. You will learn how humans moved far and wide around the globe from the birthplace of humankind in Africa.

And we're going to make some **AMAZING** discoveries along the way, about how science can help us understand the story of humankind and what being part of the human family actually means – like, no matter what skin colour we have, language we speak or place we're from, we all come from the same ancestors.

Armed with this awesome knowledge, you'll be able to bust common myths about where people come from, what race is and what it really means to be a human being. And you'll be able to tell your friends and family the epic true story of everyone who has ever lived, because you are part of that story.

WHERE ARE YOU REALLY FROM?

My name is Adam, and I'm a scientist. What I love most is learning about nature and history. When you combine these two subjects, you end up studying **EVOLUTION** — which is the history of life on Earth. I've written lots of books and I present television and radio programmes, and I love everything there is to know about science. I'm your tour guide on this epic journey, but I'm the first to admit that I — and all scientists — don't know everything. And so I have assembled a brilliant team of other excellent expert humans to help us on our way:

Emma Norry is an amazing writer of loads of books for young people who's helping me tell these stories, and Adam Ming is an artist and illustrator who creates cool and funny comics and drawings. (Yes — there are two Adams, just to confuse things!)

All three of us love telling stories, through words, science and pictures. We all have different backgrounds, and often I'll throw it over to Em to tell us about her experiences, or to Adam M

ADAM M.

because sometimes pictures do a better job than words. But the very best thing about working as a team is that we have different origins, identities and stories to tell – which means we can bring different things to this book.

ADAM R: I'm a mix of English and Guyanese Indian (my dad is from Yorkshire but grew up in New Zealand; my mother was Indian but born in Guyana in South America). I grew up in Suffolk with my dad, my stepmum (she's from Essex and her father is from Liverpool, but his dad was a Russian Jew), one sister, two stepbrothers and one half-brother. Now I live in London with my own three kids, one cat and a dog (they hate each other). I love science, cricket, superhero films and comics.

EM: I'm a mix too! I was born in Cardiff, Wales. I'm Jewish and half Caribbean. I moved around all through my childhood but now live in Bournemouth with my husband and two teenagers. I love history, cooking Thai food, reading and watching sci-fi and gangster films.

ADAM M: Hi, I'm Adam Ming and I'm going to try to make you laugh and help you learn with pictures. I learn best with pictures, and I've drawn thousands of pictures to help people say what they're **REALLY** trying to say. I'm 50% Chinese on my dad's side and on my mom's side there's a dash of English, and either Spanish or Portuguese ancestry –

nobody really knows for certain. So part of me really has no idea where I come from.

So that's us. Now what about you — where are you from? Hopefully you'll find that easy to answer. Perhaps you live in London or Tokyo or Barcelona or Paris or Berlin. But has anyone ever asked you, **'Yeah, but where are you really from?'**

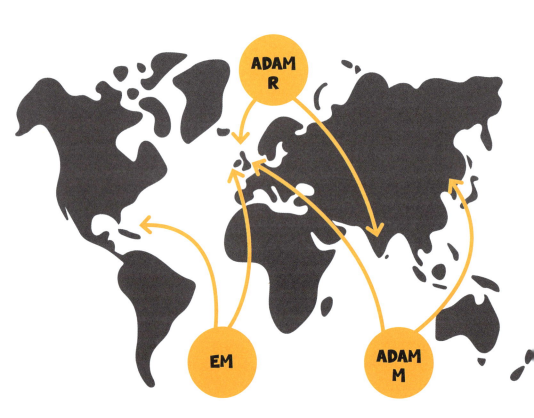

People have certainly asked me. When I was young it happened quite a lot, growing up in the middle of the countryside where there weren't very many people with brown skin like mine. Today it happens much less, but it's still a question that people ask and get asked. What does it actually mean? It's a funny sort of question to get asked because it really only happens to people whose families have come from other countries in their past, even if they were born – like in my case – here in Britain. Or if they have different features to the majority of British people. Things like skin colour, or hair colour or texture.

Only last week someone said to me that Indians are 'exotic', which is sort of nice, but also a bit weird. Because I'm not Indian, and I'm definitely not very exotic. I'm from Ipswich, which is a nice, happily boring small town in England, with a football team that I love, despite them being not brilliant (at the moment – but we are getting better every match).

Everyone's story is different, because everyone is unique, and you could answer, 'I'm from Planet Earth,' which is definitely true. People are different to each other and I think that is wonderful, because it would be extremely boring if everyone was the same. In this book, we're going to go deeeeeep into where everyone is from, and that means everyone with every skin colour or hair colour. Why? Well, the truth of where we're all really from, if we go back far enough, is much more **fascinating**, **complicated**, **weird** and **wonderful** than you could ever have imagined:

it's the story of life on Earth, and

you are a big part of it.

Because inside you,

everywhere in your body,

is the story of the

whole

of human history . . .

CHAPTER 1

A LONG TIME AGO . . .

To get us going, we need to cover some basics. So let's go back to the beginning. We're going to talk about how evolution works, and how scientists try to understand life on Earth. I want to tell the story of where you really come from. Not your home or street or town or country. But the 4 *billion* year history of evolution that results in YOU. That's a story that doesn't just involve life and evolution, but also the land, the sea, the planet, the Moon and, in fact, the whole solar system. It's the most epic story ever told, so we need to start at the very, *very* beginning.

The universe began about 13.8 billion years ago, give or take. That is a very long time, and it's quite difficult for us to compute in our heads. I did a quick calculation and worked out that if you started counting *now* at a steady pace of about one number per second and kept going without sleeping or eating, it would take about *450 years* to get to 13.8 billion. Basically, it's a *very* long time ago.

The universe started 13.8 billion years ago from nothing, a nothingness that is also pretty difficult — probably impossible — for most of us to understand. Then, with a massive

BOOM!

literally *everything* came into being. Everything that exists in the universe, all of space, time and matter, instantaneously came into being at the **Big Bang**.

THE BIG BANG

The Big Bang is one way that scientists explain how the universe started. The idea is that the Big Bang was the very first event in space and time for our universe. There wasn't anything before it, because time actually started then. This is also a pretty brain-scrambling idea, but think of it like this:

what were you like before you were born?

The answer is that you weren't like anything at all because you didn't exist. Well, the universe was born at the Big Bang, and it didn't exist before that. There are other ideas that physicists and space scientists argue about (such as whether the universe is eternal, or whether there have been many big bangs that loop over many billions of years). But THE Big Bang is what most scientists think kick-started the universe.

FUN FACT:

There is no sound in space because there is no air, and sound travels in the air, so the Big Bang didn't make much of a bang at all. It was quite big though, given that it was the event that created everything in the universe. So, definitely Big, but not much of a Bang!

THE SUN FORMS

Nothing much happened for the next 8 billion years (actually that's really not true: stars and planets and galaxies were being formed almost continuously, bathing the darkness in light, but that's not important for this story). Then about 5 billion years ago, in our galaxy – the Milky Way – a star began to form. It was a pretty insignificant star compared to the rest of the universe, but his little star would become our Sun. Huge clouds of helium and hydrogen swirled around in space like a **gigantic galactic fart**, and eventually they condensed under the force of gravity into a hot ball of fiery matter. That was the beginning of our Sun's evolution – though when it first formed, it was smaller and dimmer than it is today.

When stars form, they often have leftover bits that orbit around them, and sometimes they slowly crash into each other and can stick together. Once they get big enough, they form rocks, and then boulders, and then planetoids, and eventually they form planets – we call this process **ACCRETION**.

All the planets in our solar system formed this way. The Earth – our home – began to take shape about 4.5 billion years ago. But it didn't look much like it does today. Back then it was a proper hellish nightmare: no water, volcanic boiling rocks, no atmosphere and meteors raining down from the sky with so much force that the solid rocks would actually evaporate every few days – like smashing thin ice on a lake. If you time-travelled there, you'd be very dead as soon as your feet touched the ground. Actually, there was no ground either – just molten iron and rocks – so you'd probably be dead the moment you arrived, either vaporised, smashed by a meteor or just burnt to a crisp. None of these are great options if you ask me. The young Earth was not even remotely a place where life could exist.

THE WORST DAY EVER AND THE MOON

And if you think *that* sounds bad, things were about to get much worse. About 50 million years after the Earth formed, it had its **worst day ever**. You know how some days, it's raining and you wake up in a bad mood, there's no milk for breakfast and you haven't done your homework, and you're late for school? One of those days when everything just *sucks*?

Well, this day was much worse. A humongous rock about the same size as the planet Mars was hurtling through space. Scientists have given this rock the name Theia, which is a lovely, pretty name, and completely inappropriate because of what happened next. Theia **SMASHED** into our baby planet, and it was the biggest thing that has ever hit us. It was a glancing blow, not smack in the middle but towards the top of the planet, and it knocked the Earth so hard that it permanently shifted its vertical axis to what we have today – about 23 degrees. Most planets spin around vertically, but ours is tilted at an angle.

Every time you look at the Moon, say a little thanks to Theia — not for causing so much massively destructive havoc, but for making the planet that we live on today.

THANKS, THEIA!

A lump that got knocked off the planet in the blow was flung into space but didn't get far, because it was caught in Earth's gravity, and it wobbled around in space like a colossal rocky jelly. Like I said, worst day ever. But after some time, the rock eventually settled, rounded up and became the Moon. Today the gravitational pull of the Moon causes the tides, where life thrives, and it provides illumination for all the nocturnal creatures, like bats, badgers, foxes and security guards. And the tilt of the Earth's axis is also what causes the seasons. So even though Theia caused such an incredibly destructive event, it also set up the planet that we enjoy today.

As the Earth goes round, the angle at which the Sun hits parts of the Earth changes. That's why we get more heat in the summer because we're angled closer to the Sun. Both the Moon and the Sun are crucial for life to exist.

COMET RAIN

For about 300 million years after Theia, Earth was still a pretty awful place. Meteors and comets rained down from space so often that the land and the oceans would vaporise every few weeks. And the surface was molten and constantly changing. Geologists (people who study rocks and planets) call this time period the Hadean, named after Hades, the Greek version of hell. Basically, **WORST HOLIDAY DESTINATION EVER**.

WORST HOLIDAY EVER

HADEAN PERIOD

EARTH

This didn't happen overnight — we're dealing with timescales that are totally incomprehensible to us — but then eventually, it all just calmed down. The meteors stopped falling from space and the land began to form as the oceans settled and cooled. This was about 3.9 billion years ago. And as soon as the Earth was a bit more chill, and things stabilised, life began. How can we possibly know this? Well, we've found fossilised cells — tiny rings embedded in ancient rocks — which are almost that old.

LUCA – THE GRANDMOTHER OF *ALL LIVING THINGS*

Now, we definitely don't know this for sure, but some scientists (including me) think that life began at the very bottom of the ocean. Other scientists think that it started on the surface, where there is light and lightning. Some people even think that it came from space! But in science we try to come up with explanations that fit what we can see and what we can test.

Did life start on the Earth's surface with light and lightning providing the spark? I don't think that's a good explanation because most life today doesn't need light to live, and lightning generally has the effect of frazzling living things, which is not helpful for having a nice day. As for space, well, it's a fun idea, but it doesn't actually answer the question of how life got started. It just moves the origin of life to another place, so it's very good for comics and movies, but not so good for the average scientist.

I think the ocean is the best explanation for the origin of life, because deep down in the sea there is a location where the rocks and sparkling gases behave a bit like living cells. Gases and chemicals bubble up from the sea floor in huge towers that are filled with tiny holes and nooks and crannies. It's a very bustling environment, full of energy with heat and gases and nutrients. I think that this is the best explanation of how the first cells came to be, because that is similar to how cells work today — energy, heat, food, all encapsulated in tiny pockets, a bit like a cell in your body. But I could be wrong, and one day we will have a better idea of how life got started on Earth, as we look for more evidence and do more experiments.

Scientists love being wrong. What do you think happened?

SCIENTISTS DON'T KNOW EVERYTHING

People often think that scientists know everything, but that's not true. Most scientists are hard-working, and think about their work very carefully, but we don't know everything at all. Science is about finding answers and sometimes those answers might not be right. But that is absolutely fine. The most important thing a scientist can say is '**I DON'T KNOW**'. I say 'we don't know' throughout this book, and you should never be afraid to say to a teacher or friend that you don't know an answer. Who knows – one day, you might be the scientist who finds out the answer to one of these questions. And then you can tell me the answer to something I've been wondering about for years.

So we're not exactly sure what that first life form was like, but we do know a few things about it. The first life form was just a single cell, maybe a little bit like **BACTERIA** today — too small to see without a microscope, but buzzing with chemical activity.

We call it LUCA, which stands for the '**L**ast **U**niversal **C**ommon **A**ncestor'. Think about it like this: when you look at your family, your parents are your most recent ancestors, but they are only the ancestors of their own children. Your grandmother is the ancestor of you and your parent and all her grandchildren.

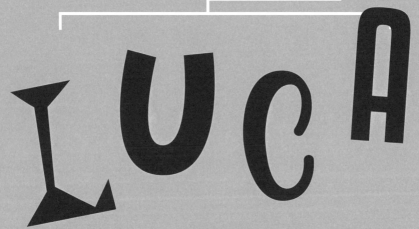

LUCA is the grandmother of **EVERY LIVING THING THAT HAS EVER EXISTED ON THE WHOLE PLANET**.

That includes you, your pet cat or dog or hamster, the broccoli in your fridge, that tree out the window, that bit of mould on some bread that you should probably throw away, the bird that did a poo on your mum's car last night and the bacteria in that poo . . . **EVERYTHING!**

TREES OF LIFE

At least as far as we know, all life that we're aware of is on the big family tree that has LUCA at its root. What we don't know, and maybe never will, is if there have been other trees that started but didn't survive. Some scientists have suggested that there may even be another family tree of living things today that we've never detected! I'm not one of them though, and I think that's a fun but silly idea. But my challenge to you is become a scientist and **PROVE ME WRONG**!

LUCA was very different from us — obviously — a tiny gloopy cell growing in hot rocks at the bottom of a bubbly ocean. But we think it had some features in common with the cells we have within our own bodies. LUCA had genes, made of DNA. DNA contains the instructions needed for a life form to develop, function and reproduce. It's a long, stringy molecule and each piece of information is carried on a different section of it. These sections are genes. You will discover more about these clever things in the next chapter.

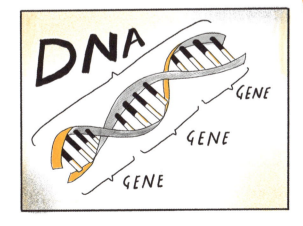

LUCA also probably had a cell membrane, an outer layer a bit like skin, that lets substances go in and out of it. And we think it had a **METABOLISM** – basically, a way of eating and turning food into energy. LUCA took chemicals out of the water and converted them into food, and therefore energy, and that's how it lived. Eating is something all living things need to do, and we think that LUCA did it first. But remember this: nothing else was alive at the time of LUCA, so whatever it was eating, it wasn't the food we eat today. It was just stuff floating around in a volcanic vent. No sandwiches, curries, burgers or crisps. Just . . . stuff.

BIOLOGICAL RULE BOOK

One of the basic rules of biology is that all living things are made of cells. Cells are the basic units of life, have lots of different functions that keep us alive and are so tiny we need a microscope to see them. They can be different sizes and shapes, and we're made up of roughly 100 trillion cells. (Actually that's not true. I'm roughly 40 trillion cells. **YOU** are probably fewer than that because I'm guessing you're not an adult man, so maybe more like 20 trillion cells. But we don't really know as they are so tiny, it's not easy to count them.)

Another rule of biology is that cells can only be born from an existing cell. New cells can't come from things that aren't cells. Every cell that has ever existed came about when its parent split and divided to make new cells. So when you graze your knee in the park or one of your baby teeth falls out, the cells that patch up the hole have grown out of another cell, which itself grew out of another cell, which grew from another cell.

This might hurt your brain but you can keep going back until that cell is the egg inside your mum, which came from another cell, which came from another cell, which came from a cell, which . . . and so on and so on. If you do that for about 4 billion years, you can get all the way back to LUCA. There is one exception to this rule, and that is LUCA.

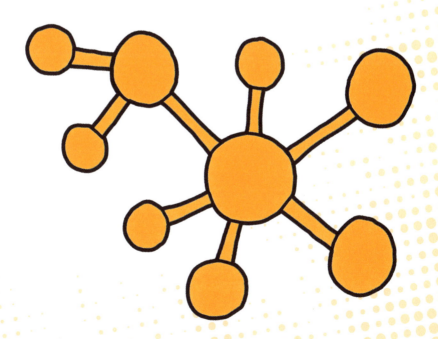

Over billions of years life has evolved and adapted, from the earliest microbes to the richness and range of life forms we see on our planet today. But rewind back to the very beginning and it's LUCA that is the original ancestor of all living things.

So the first answer to the question 'Where are you *really* from?' is . . . some tiny gloopy cells trapped inside boiling rock at the bottom of the sea. Sorry, guys.

CHAPTER 2

ADAPT OR DIE!

That was only the beginning. After LUCA, the Earth was very much alive and the seas were bursting with life. But only with tiny single-cell **ORGANISMS** such as bacteria and their very similar but different cousins called archaea (say: AR-KAY-YA).

STUFF WAS HAPPENING BUT IT WAS STILL PRETTY BORING.

But just like an acorn can grow into a huge oak tree, or Peter Parker can transform into Spider-Man, small weedy things can become incredible. About 2 billion years ago, the cells stopped being just single cells and started to clump together into blobs of cells — the first **MULTICELLULAR** organisms. Hundreds of millions of years later, those blobs became pads of cells shaped like flat discs, which could float on the seas. They still needed to eat, though — even a blob gets hungry. So how do we evolve from a pancake to something more like an animal?

If you're flat as a pancake and floating on the sea, then it's not easy to eat. Basically, you just have to wait for dinner to float by. Imagine if you had to eat not by putting food in your mouth and swallowing, but by just lying on top of it. (Note: please do not try this at the dinner table. Or at least if you do, please don't blame me.) A better way to trap food is if you're a tube.

Once you're a tube shape, you can trap food and hold on to it. You've also got the ability to take food in at one end and let out waste at the other: in other words, an extremely important stage in the evolution of life on Earth was when living things grew a mouth and also a bum.

Mouths and bums are incredibly important, and pretty much all animals today have both. But back then you're still a floating mouth and bum, waiting for food to drift into your mouth. If you can move, though, you can go after lunch instead of waiting for it to come to you, so wriggling or having fins might allow you to swim around. Plus, being able to move is also a good way to avoid being eaten.

What else might be useful for finding food? How about being able to detect food by sniffing it out? When you're walking down the street and your nose detects the smell from a chip shop, it's telling you where to get some delicious dinner. Having senses is a real advantage in seeking out food. Being able to see what you might want to eat is pretty handy too — so about **500 MILLION YEARS AGO**, some unknown sea creatures evolved to have vision. At first it was just a few cells on the head of a tiny wormy creature that could detect sunlight. Soon enough, that developed into a little pit of cells on its head that could detect light from different directions. And before long, clear cells sat on top of those light-detecting cells, focusing the light, creating a lens. And after a few million years, eyes were all over the animal kingdom in the seas. Creatures were swimming

around and they could now see their food and go after it. Plus, they could keep an eye out for predators who wanted to eat them too.

Because those creatures could see food and escape from predators more easily, they would have had more babies. That is what evolution is really about: having babies who have the highest chance of surviving, so that they can have babies and so on and so on, making sure life carries on.

It's a madly huge idea, that our senses – **sight, sound, smell, taste and touch** – started out hundreds of millions of years ago with an unknown wormy thing wriggling about in the seas.

We get this type of information from looking at fossils. We can see the eyes of early animals that died more than half a billion years ago. We compare their fossilised remains with living creatures so we can work out what were legs or fins for moving around, or eyes or antennae for the senses, or mouths and bums for eating and pooing.

But those aren't the only pieces of evidence available to us today. In the last few years, our understanding of the story of life on Earth has been radically rewritten with the addition of another piece of evidence that literally everybody and every living thing carries inside them – a magnificent molecule called DNA. All life forms from different classes and categories share this common ingredient. So let's take a quick DNA detour before we get back to life on Earth and the story of you.

THE DISGUSTING STORY OF DNA

DNA stands for deoxyribonucleic acid (take a deep breath and say: DEE-OXY-RYE-BO-NEW-CLAY-ICK acid). Learn it - people will think you're clever if you can say it, I promise.

It's one of the most important molecules in the whole of biology, because it is a code that contains all the instructions to make an organism. We'll come to that in a minute, but first, the story of the discovery of DNA is really interesting, in the sense that it is absolutely, **TOTALLY DISGUSTING**. DNA was first discovered by a Swiss scientist called Friedrich Miescher. He was working in a German hospital in the nineteenth century during a war, and the wards were full of soldiers with really nasty wounds — bullet holes and stab wounds from being in close combat with their enemies. Doctors in those days didn't know much about infections or how to keep injuries clean, so the wounds were often infected, smelly and rotting, which is both **sad and entirely gross**.

Miescher had an idea, though, which was both genius and revolting. Take the used bandages, soaked through with pus and blood, and try to find out what was in the *juice*.

After months of careful work, Miescher isolated a molecule that was only found in the centre of cells — the nucleus — so he called it *nuclein*. What he had actually discovered was DNA. But he didn't know what it was and was super busy, so he left the samples and never really looked at them again. **DNA wasn't really purified again for another 50 years.**

DNA DISCOVERY . . . NEARLY!

DR MIESCHER, WHAT ARE YOU DOING? HAVE YOU LOST SOMETHING?

I'M LOOKING FOR A BANDAGE

OH DEAR. YOU POOR THING. DON'T WORRY — I'LL GO AND GET YOU ONE

THANK YOU, NURSE. JUST MAKE SURE IT'S SOAKED IN PUS AND BLOOD!

But the story doesn't end there. In the 1940s, people became interested in what **DNA** was doing in a nucleus. Some scientists discovered that you could take **DNA** from one cell and put it in a different cell, and that second cell would take on the properties of the first cell, as if borrowing Ronaldo's football boots suddenly made you as good as him at scoring goals. It was from here that people began to work out that **DNA** was the key ingredient for telling a cell what to be and how to behave. Even more importantly, they wanted to know how it got copied from cell to cell as they divided.

This became one of the biggest quests in the history of science – to figure out how **DNA** could hold information and pass from cell to cell every time a cell divided. By the 1950s, lots of different scientists were getting closer to understanding how **DNA** does this trick, but it was the combined efforts of three scientists who cracked it. Rosalind Franklin had taken a very special type of photograph of **DNA** using an X-ray, which meant it was possible to work out the shape of **DNA**. Two scientists called Francis Crick and James Watson got hold of this photo (without Franklin's knowledge!) and used it to work out that **DNA** is what's known as a

double helix.

IMAGINE A LADDER, AND TWIST IT ROUND LIKE A CORKSCREW — THAT'S THE SHAPE OF DNA.

They worked out that this double shape is how **DNA** works. Think of it like this: if you did a drawing of yourself, but cut it in half and gave the two halves to someone else, they could fill in the other halves to make two whole versions of the drawing again. You have duplicated yourself.

That's roughly how **DNA** works too. All the information is kept in the rungs of the ladder, and every time a cell divides, the double helix splits in two and replaces the missing half, so you end up with two bits of identical **DNA** when before you only had one.

Working this out was completely genius, and Crick and Watson got the Nobel Prize for this in 1962. Sadly, Franklin had already died, and Watson had been pretty sexist and mean to her because she was a woman. But nowadays we know that it was her genius as well that led to the discovery of how **DNA** copies itself.

AN INSTRUCTION MANUAL FOR LIFE

Inside you (and all other animals and plants), all your **DNA** sits in a little bag in the middle of your cells, kind of like the head teacher's office, where a whole school is run from. The nucleus contains all the instructions on how to make a **YOU**.

INSTRUCTIONS ON HOW TO MAKE A YOU

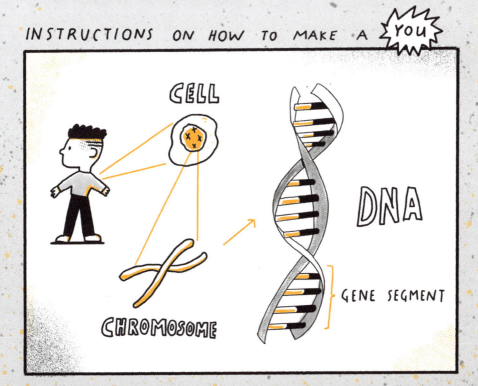

CELL

CHROMOSOME

DNA

GENE SEGMENT

DNA carries all the information for life and we need it to survive, grow and multiply. You can think of it almost like an extremely long and stringy set of cooking instructions. And if you want to know how long: if you typed out all of your DNA, it would fill about *21,000* books the same size as this one, but it is so small that it is packaged up inside your cells. We call the total amount of DNA in your cells the **GENOME**.

Your genome is organised into sections called *chromosomes.* **You have 46 chromosomes in every cell, 23 from your mother and 23 from your father**, and on each chromosome there are important nuggets of information, which we call genes. These are the bits of data that influence everything from your eye colour to how tall you are, or even whether your ear wax is sticky or flakey — basically all the information to make a YOU. It is all pretty complicated, but maybe think about it like this: this whole book is your genome, each chapter is a chromosome, and each sentence is a gene. The whole book only makes sense when you read all the sentences.

Now, because you get half your genes from your biological mum and half from your biological dad, that's why you probably look more like them than some random person you've never met before. Your genes are a mix of your parents' genes.

And your parents got their genes from their parents, who got theirs from their parents, and so on and so on – all the way back through time, through all of your ancestors and all of their ancestors. This goes back in a perfect unbroken chain to the beginning of life on Earth itself. LUCA had genes 3.9 billion years ago and passed them on to every living thing that has existed since.

Humans have about 20,000 genes. Which isn't that many – it's more than cats, but less than a banana, or rice, or even a tiny water flea! But in us, they all work together to make something as excellent and clever as **YOU**.

43

LIFE-CHAMGING SPELLNG ERRRORS

Because we now know that DNA is passed down from parent to child, and that has been going on for billions of years, we can get back to our story of life on Earth and how we get to you. LUCA had genes and so do you, but you may have noticed that you are not a single cell living in a volcanic rock. In the billions of years after life began, it evolved and became more and more complex.

Evolution is the process of how **SPECIES** change over time. It doesn't mean one creature changes during its lifetime; it means the children of one species might be ever so slightly different to their parents, and *their* children might be a teeny bit different again. If they keep changing like this over dozens or hundreds of generations, then one species will slowly change into another.

If those changes mean that the children are better hunters, or can fight off disease, or can eat different foods that grow near where they live, they might survive longer and have more babies themselves. We call this **ADAPTATION**: the species has adapted to the environment and been selected by nature to survive. The way this process happens in nature is slow and gradual over many generations.

Lots of names in science are completely incomprehensible (like *deoxyribonucleic acid*). Others are quite fun, like black holes (which, by the way, aren't black and aren't even holes). Some names are just useful and say exactly what they do. That's why we call the way life has changed on Earth **EVOLUTION BY NATURAL SELECTION**.

When DNA is copied and passed on to a new cell, the copying is not always perfect. Occasionally, an error can creep in. Say you were using the picture of you cut in half, but the next person to fill in the missing half accidently drew an ear on. Now you've got a drawing of a person with one ear. Next, you cut that in half and pass it on, and the person who gets the half with the ear just goes, 'Oh well, there's an ear on this half so I'd better draw an ear on the other side too.'

But now you've got two ears! You've evolved.

Sometimes we think of these random copying errors in our DNA as spelling mistakes. Sometimes those mistakes just make no sense at all, but once in a while they can change the word to a different one with a different meaning.

TRY THIS: I'm going to turn a meerkat into a dead cat in four moves, by changing one letter at a time.

meer kat

deer kat

dear kat

dead kat

dead cat

Each step makes new words that are real, but I've completely changed the meaning.

That's the idea behind how creatures evolve. DNA changes with spelling mistakes from generation to generation, and as they accumulate over millions of years, the creature can change from one species to another. It's **insanely** more complex than mutating a meerkat into a dead cat in four moves, but you get the picture.

EVOLUTION ISN'T ALWAYS SUCCESSFUL . . .

For us, with our **100,000 _books_ of DNA** in each cell, we can now look at what is the same in us and what is different. The DNA of any two people differs by a tiny teeny amount, much less than 1%, but because our genomes are so big, that's enough to encode the difference between you and me and everyone else. And nowadays we can look so closely at our DNA, and the DNA of all sorts of animals, that we can work out when those spelling mistakes happened and how one creature evolved into another.

By the way, the difference between your DNA and a chimpanzee's is **only about 4%**, which doesn't seem like much, but I think you are probably quite different from a chimp. Your parents may disagree.

THE 'PERFECT' MATCH

CHAPTER 3

FROM AMMONITES
TO ZEPHYROSAURUS

Now that you know all about DNA, let's get back to the story of life on Earth, and we're going to start racing through it now. About 450 million years ago, there were fishy things and wormy things and armour-plated things. But for reasons we don't really understand, animal evolution then went completely crazy. Loads of new species suddenly (that is: over millions of years) turned up and the whole evolution of animals kicked off in the seas. Skip forward a few more tens of millions of years and you have the rise of the reptiles. And another 100 million years later, **the dinosaurs arrived**. Then finally, 3 million years ago, humans finally came on the scene. Ready to meet some of these scaly/scary/hairy looking creatures?

Let's start 450 million years ago in the sea. We've got millions of fossils of the creatures that lived in the oceans back then, including a lot of **TRILOBITES** (say: TRY-LO-BITES) and **AMMONITES**. Trilobites, were among the oldest animals that ever lived. They were what's known as **ARTHROPODS**, a bit like insects and spiders, as you can see from their segmented bodies. Ammonites were marine creatures too, and like trilobites, are now extinct. Their nearest 'relatives' now would be the octopus and cuttlefish, but that just shows how evolution can change one thing into something completely different over a long enough time. During this time period, there would also have been jellyfish and sea urchins. And giant armour-plated fish with terrifying bony faces and enormous built-in fangs – **DUNKLEOSTEUS** (say: DUNK-LEE-OSS-TEE-USS).

Fish suck oxygen out of the water it's dissolved in, but (*you may have noticed*) we don't. We fill our chests with air, and in the depths of our lungs, oxygen enters our cells. All animals for the first few hundred million years breathed underwater, but then one day, about 350 million years ago, fishy-type creatures evolved so that they could gasp air instead of extracting the water with gills. Some of them would hang out in shallow rock pools, splashing around and wading, exactly like you might do at the beach.

Most fish don't have necks, and (*you may also have noticed*) we do. But there was one very special type of animal that evolved neck muscles, which enabled it to lift its big, flat head out of the water. And it had fins that were muscly enough for it to waddle a bit. This was an animal that made the first step . . . on to land. We call it **TIKTAALIK** — and it was about the size of a sausage dog. This little sausage was a big step in the evolution of life on Earth — this time, actually on *earth*.

RISE OF THE RAMPANT REPTILES

Now, there have been literally billions of different types of animal on Earth over the last few million years, so we're going to have to skip over a few. But once animals began to live on land and breathe air, they thrived and evolved and diversified, and they started to look like reptiles, which laid eggs. Some ate other animals (**CARNIVORES**), others ate plants (**HERBIVORES**), and others ate the eggs of other reptiles (**OVIVORES**). See if you can guess what **INSECTIVORES** ate? That's right! Insects!

Skip forward again, and we meet some animals that you will be very familiar with. After another 100 million years or so, the first **DINOSAURS** evolved.

There were thousands of types of dinosaur and many other **PREHISTORIC** creatures living alongside them— all of them on land. The ones that flew, such as Pterodactyl (TERRO-DAK-TIL), were actually flying reptiles, and the ones that swam, like Plesiosaurs (PLEH-SEE-OH-SAWS), were marine reptiles. They were all around for ages, about 150 million years, and flourished during that time.

Other big changes were happening too. The land was changing shape. While the dinosaurs were around, the Earth split from being one giant land mass surrounded by sea into separate areas. We call this time the **MESOZOIC** (say: MEE-ZO-ZO-ICK) period, and it lasted for so long that we've broken it up into three main chunks.

TRIASSIC (TRI-ASS-SIC) 252.17 to 201.3 million years ago: During the late Triassic period, dinosaurs were about the same size as the largest mammals living today. This time brought us the first dinosaurs and flying reptiles.

JURASSIC (You know how to pronounce that – thanks, movies) 201.3 to 145 million years ago: During this time, dinosaurs developed into huge GIANTS. They grew so big because of what they ate and their bone structure. Also, oxygen levels in the air were much higher, and this allowed them to maintain bigger bodies.

CRETACEOUS (CRUH-TAY-SHUS) 145 to 66 million years ago: This was the golden age of the dinosaurs we all know and love – Tyrannosaurus rex, Spinosaurus, Triceratops – and the beginning of the bird-like dinosaurs, like Archeopteryx (AR-KEE-OP-THE-RIX). But it ended, 66 million years ago, with a mass extinction caused by a massive asteroid smashing into Earth, and many animals became extinct.

Some birds survived, though, which means the birds you see in the sky are the direct descendants of dinosaurs. NOTE: almost all of the amazing dinosaurs and sea beasts in the *Jurassic World* films are NOT from the Jurassic period at all. They are actually almost all from the Cretaceous period. So it really should be called Cretaceous Park. Suck it, Spielberg!

CRETACEOUS PARK

THE END

But that wasn't the end of it. The asteroid also produced a tsunami – an **ABSOLUTELY GIGANTIC WAVE**, so big that it washed around the whole world – and the explosion threw up a dust cloud that blotted out the Sun for hundreds of years. It was game over for the dinosaurs. The big ones died, whole ecosystems collapsed and life on Earth radically changed, again.

Here's an important thing. We are not descended from dinosaurs. I know that would be really cool, but the mammals and dinosaurs had already split by 200 million years ago. Think of it like this: say you've got a brother. You and your brother have got the same parents. But your brother has children, and then you have children one day, so they are cousins with each other. And say your brother's children have children, and they have children, and after a thousand years they got hairier and shorter and started walking on all fours. But your kids and grandchildren stay roughly like you are for the next thousand years. If this happened, your descendants would be a different species from your brother's descendants. You have a common ancestor — your parents — but his descendants and yours have evolved to be different species.

The mammals and dinosaurs were already cousins by the time the asteroid hit and they lived alongside each other. (The carnivorous dinosaurs probably ate quite a lot of mammals too.)

These mammals started small, though some were pretty grizzly looking: stocky hairy beasts, a bit like chunky otters, but much less friendly. **(The carnivorous mammals probably ate quite a lot of baby dinosaurs, so everything's fair again.)**

Lots of animals did survive the asteroid, though. For example, crocodiles survived, but dinosaurs didn't. Plesiosaurs died, but sharks survived. We genuinely don't know why. But crucially for our story, the mammals survived. And now we're getting closer to the story of humans, and of YOU.

MAMMALS MULTIPLY

By this time there were many different types of mammal, from mouse-like shrews to small dog-sized creatures and stumpy ponies. Over the next tens of millions of years, the mammals continued to grow and spread around the globe. Life on Earth has a habit of evolving into new areas so it can find food to eat and safety from being eaten. Some mammals took to the skies – and became bats – and others went back into the water – whales and dolphins. Some went into the forests, and some went up trees.

About 60 million years ago, we see the first of the **PRIMATES**. At first, they were a bit like lemurs with long tails, but soon enough (that is, millions of years later) they became more like monkeys and gibbons. Then, 10 million years ago, some of these monkeys evolved to become the family that would eventually become the **GREAT APES**, and YOU, my friend, *are a great ape*.

Along with gorillas, chimps, orangutans and bonobos, humans are great apes, and all five of those types of ape evolved from a common ancestor. Ten million years ago there were probably even more species than that, but we don't really know exactly who the ancestor of all the great apes was. What we *do* know is that these are the ones who have survived today.

So, it's time to meet more of your hairy ape ancestors . . .

Some great apes stayed in trees, but some made nests in the ground. The bodies of all of these great apes changed over evolution, depending on the lives they were living. Remember adaptation? Well, being able to swing through trees is easier if you've got very long bendy arms. Walking on the ground is easier if you're on all fours with chunky knuckles and your head positioned so you can hold it up when you're galloping. But some of them evolved to stand up on their back legs. If you can stand up tall, you can wade in water, you can keep a lookout over hedges and grasslands for hungry lions that might want to eat you, and you can do things with your hands, like make tools, carry babies or throw spears (or pick your nose while you're walking). **Maybe 4 million years ago or so, some of those great apes took a big step . . .**

ONE GIANT STEP FOR HUMANKIND . . .

Evolution is full of big steps, but this one was a giant leap. Our ancestors had become **BIPEDS** — walking on two feet. Actually, lots of animals walk on two feet — meerkats, chimps and gorillas can too, but they can't do it for long. We are **HABITUAL BIPEDS**, which means we only walk on two feet. Our ancestors evolved this ability about 4 million years ago and have remained two-footed ever since.

If we were to look at your skeleton, but it was all jumbled up, we could pick out your foot bones and your leg bones, and we could work out things about your body and how you moved when you weren't just a skeleton. By just looking at the shape of your feet and the position of your legs, we can tell that you were a biped. We can see this in the fossilised bones of ancient humans too: they have flatter feet than other apes, and their leg bones look like they come straight down from their hip bones, and their skulls sit on top of the bodies, instead of coming forward like a chimp's or gorilla's.

In a place called Laetoli in Tanzania, Africa, we have even discovered the fossilised **footprints** of a person strolling along with their kid next to them. They were probably in warm, soft volcanic mud, maybe holding hands, like you might do walking on a beach with your mum or dad. Those footprints were made more than **3 million years ago**, but they dried and set and have remained preserved all that time, and today they provide us with clues about our ancestors. We're not sure what species was walking in that soft mud, but many scientists think it was one that we've named **Australopithecus afarensis** (OSS-TRALLO-PITHY-CUS AFF-AREN-SIS).

From then on, though, the great apes who are our ancestors had arrived. They weren't quite like us yet — mostly a bit shorter and chunkier, and almost certainly much hairier — but they *were* a species of human. They also had smaller heads and smaller brains than us — we are very clever, of course, but we have unusually large brains compared to our nearest cousins.

Over the next few millions of years, there were a few types of different human species, all over the world. There was one we call **HOMO ERECTUS** – upright people – and the tiny people in Indonesia we call **HOMO FLORESIENSIS** (FLOH-REZY-ENSIS: these people have been nicknamed the hobbits, because they were short and had big feet; we don't actually know if they had hairy feet like a hobbit, but I think it's OK to pretend they did).

In Europe, there were the **NEANDERTHALS** (*Homo neanderthalensis* – NEE-ANDER-TARL-ENSIS), who looked very much like us but had even bigger heads and broad chests.

NEANDERTHAL

DENISOVAN

And there were the **DENISOVANS** (DE-NEES-OVANS), who lived in what is now Siberia in Russia and East Asia, but we don't really know what they looked like, because so far we've only found a tooth and a finger bone from a teenage girl.

Our species, **HOMO SAPIENS**, evolved in Africa about half a million years ago. The earliest known members lived 315,000 years ago in what is now Morocco in North Africa, but we've found the bones of other *Homo sapiens* in other places in Africa, including countries in the east, such as Ethiopia. We've only got their fossilised bones, but if we reconstruct them, their bodies were pretty much the same as people today. If you met one of these people on a bus or in the park, they'd look just like everyone else — that is, if you tidied them up, gave them a haircut and dressed them in some modern clothes.

HOMO SAPIEN

KEEP ON MOVING!

Humans have always moved, travelled and explored new lands. During the time our species was *only* in Africa, we moved around on that massive continent, maybe following the seasons or hunting down migrating animals. Then, around 80,000 years ago, some *Homo sapiens* started to move out of Africa and into Asia and Europe. This wasn't migration like we think about it today — where people move country to change jobs or to be with family, or sometimes to escape war or persecution. Over hundreds of years, they just slowly inched out of Africa. And just to be clear, scientists call this the Out of Africa theory.

Most people remained in Africa, but the ones who began moving away evolved to look a bit different. The most obvious example is that our African ancestors 100,000 years ago probably had darker skin than most White British people today. But at some point, pale skin evolved. We think it's an adaptation to the fact that it's not as sunny in most of Europe compared to Africa, and lighter skin is better for getting vitamin D working in cloudy weather.

This is an example of a local adaptation. A **LOCAL ADAPTATION** means that as we moved into new places, with different food and weather, the bodies of our ancestors slowly changed so that we could survive better and live well in those new places.

These fine-tuned adaptations evolved to help us to survive environments on our diverse planet. Have you noticed that planets in *Star Wars* (and other science-fiction films) are all one type of ecosystem? There's an ice planet, or a desert planet, or a swamp planet, or an ocean planet. Well, Planet Earth is all of those and more. So humans evolved in different places suited to what the local environment was like.

Our success as humans — why we've not been wiped out yet — comes from moving round the planet and adapting to those environments. Imagine an

early human. If they were a good hunter, they'd have a better chance of keeping their belly full, compared to a neighbour who always came home empty-handed. It makes sense that if they ate well, they'd live longer. If they lived longer, then they'd have more chance of having children and passing on their genes. But hunting on the plains of Asia is not the same as fishing on the coast of Greenland. So maybe evolving an adaptation to like a fishy diet there would be more advantageous than evolving to like a meaty one.

Today we can extract DNA out of some fossils, which means we can get a lot of information about those people who've been dead for centuries. We can also look at the DNA of living people in those areas. We can tell if they were best suited to eating a lot of fish, or meat, or other foods. We can make clever guesses at what colour their skin was, and their eye colour too. We can't know for sure, but with our current understanding of genes and skin colour we can make rough estimates.

We can also tell interesting things about families, and who they met as they were travelling. And a few years ago, we found out something absolutely incredible. When *Homo sapiens* came to Europe about 45,000 years ago, they met the Neanderthals, who had been living there for tens of thousands of years. They were a species of human who are now extinct – the last Neanderthal bones found were about 40,000 years old, and since we haven't found any more recent ones, we think they all died about then. We've found a lot of Neanderthal fossils now, and we've put together models of what they looked like based on their bones. They had a very distinctive face, a bit chunkier than ours, with a heavier brow and a wide nose. In 2010, scientists managed to get DNA out of the arm bone of a Neanderthal man who died in a cave in Germany 40,000 years ago. And they read the DNA, just like we can with living people today. When they compared Neanderthal DNA with living human DNA, they found that almost all European people today have a little bit of Neanderthal DNA in their genomes too. Which means …

It's time to meet your ancestors again. Yes, Neanderthals were our ancestors too! They were our cousins for a long time, maybe half a million years, and *Homo sapiens* didn't meet them for a long time. But when *Homo sapiens* arrived in Europe, they met the Neanderthals and had families with them.

We now know that pretty much all light-skinned people today have some Neanderthal DNA — I do, because I've looked, and it's about 2% of my total genome. If you are light-skinned and from Europe, **your great great (and keep going about 1,600 times) grandfather or grandmother was a Neanderthal**!

The same thing happened when *Homo sapiens* reached Asia, and they met the Denisovans. Even though we've only got a tooth and a little finger bone from one teenage Denisovan girl, scientists managed to extract her genome out of the finger too. When we compare that DNA to living people today, we see that people from East Asia have Denisovan DNA. **So if you or your family are from East Asia, then your great great (and keep going about 1,600 times) grandfather or grandmother was a Denisovan!**

People from Africa (or from families with recent African ancestors) have a small but measurable bit of Neanderthal DNA, but don't tend to have Denisovan DNA, because the Denisovans didn't live in Africa at that time. But since then, people from all over the world have moved and migrated and made families and shared our ancestry from our deep, deep past. If you think your family tree is a muddle, the family tree of humankind is a total and totally **AWESOME** mess.

WHAT DOES IT ALL MEAN?

What this means is that although we might all look different to each other, we are still one species — the last remaining human species — *Homo sapiens* — us.

My youngest daughter is eight years old at the moment, and she once asked me, **'Who was the first person on Earth?'** A perfectly sensible question, but a very tricky one to answer. There wasn't really a first person, just groups of people, spread all over Africa. They'd become more like how we are today and less like their own hairy ancestors. Families are messy and complicated, and they move and start other families, and evolve very slowly. Who knows — in the future, maybe you could be the first person on Mars, but there wasn't ever really a first person on Earth. We didn't arrive; **WE EVOLVED**.

It's the DNA that is changing and that makes physical changes in bodies, and if those changes are helpful for survival, they become part of us. So over time we see evolution changing families and species.

Evolution is slow — it happens over thousands and millions of years. Creatures migrate to find food or follow warm weather, or they just move around to find shelter. We might be the only species of human alive now, but there were plenty of different types of human all over the world within the last few hundreds of thousands of years, and we evolved from a mix of different early human beings from around the African continent.

Then we slowly migrated all over the world.

You are a tiny branch on the biggest tree of all — the huge sprawling messy tree of life. You can trace your ancestry back through your family, through our species, and through the great apes and monkeys and ratty mammals, and reptiles and waddling amphibians and fishy things, and floaty blobs with eyes and fins, and single-celled things. And because all life is on the same tree, with the same type of DNA, and all part of evolution, we can eventually get all the way back to LUCA, your great great great great great great great great great great (and a few million more) grandmother, almost 4 billion years ago, at the bottom of the ocean.

Oh, and we started with A for ammonites, so let's finish with a lovely dinosaur which was alive 100–125 million years ago: **Z for ZEPHYROSAURUS** — specially for you.

EVOLUTION IN PRACTICE!

CHAPTER 4

ONE BIG MASSIVE TWISTY TREE OF LIFE

Life has existed on Earth for almost 4 billion years, but humans have only been around for a teeny fraction of that time. If you squashed the existence of our planet into just one year, starting on 1 January, then there's nothing alive at all until about February, when LUCA appears. Life on Earth stays roughly the same until July, when things get a bit more **COMPLEX, LUMPIER AND MULTICELLULAR**, and then by late September, animals are getting a bit wormy. There are no plants on the land until November, and even then they're just shrubs, at best — trees won't be around until the beginning of December. Insects are next and sharks a couple of days later. The dinosaurs turn up in mid-December but are wiped out by a big asteroid on Boxing Day. By the morning of 31 December, there are a few apes but no sign of humans yet. Our species rocks up at about 11.20pm on New Year's Eve. And you? Well, if right now is midnight on New Year's Eve, then you were born about one second ago.

But we'll come to that timeline in more detail in a couple of pages. First, we've got to think about how scientists think about life.

That 4-billion-year journey has meant that there are millions of different types of organisms on Earth, which poses a bit of a problem. Scientists like me work with so many different types of animal and plant — all with the same type of DNA — that we have to give them names which can help us identify them. We like putting things in categories because grouping things together makes it easier for us to understand the biology that we share. Categorising things helps us understand how **organisms** are related to each other and how life got to be the way it is today.

When we're trying to organise different types of organisms, we call them **SPECIES**. Each species is unique, but all life on Earth is related on the same family tree, and closely related species have lots of similarities. These similarities mean we can lump them together. All humans today are one species. All cats are one species. But house cats and tigers are not, even though they are closely related and part of the bigger cat family.

Grouping things together is called

CLASSIFICATION

Think about sitting in front of the TV trying to decide what to watch. You might want to watch the BBC, or Channel 4, or Netflix, or Disney Plus. All of the programmes are split up into sections: kids' TV is grouped together in one list, documentaries in another, the adult drama shows in another area. And within those sections, there are further groups such as TV programmes based on books, or cartoons, or superhero films. Within those sections, things will be broken down even more – such as family, horror, sci-fi, action, thriller, romance. Eventually, after wading through all of that, you might finally find a film or TV show that you actually want to watch!

When we classify things in biology, we work in a similar way, and to understand this, we're going to work our way down, from top to bottom.

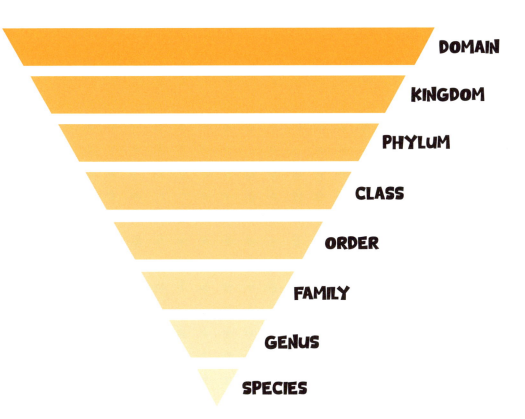

DOMAIN

KINGDOM

PHYLUM

CLASS

ORDER

FAMILY

GENUS

SPECIES

The top level is called the **domain**, and within this there are only three categories. Think of them like Netflix, Disney Plus and BBC iPlayer. In biology, the three domains are called bacteria, archaea (say: AR-KAYA) and eukaryotes (say: YOU-CARRY-OATES). Bacteria and archaea are tiny single-celled organisms, and even though they are invisible to the naked eye, they make up most of life on Earth. In fact — and you might need to sit down for this fact . . .

You have more bacterial cells on you and in you than you have human cells!

This, by the way, is totally normal, and we need them to survive, so don't be too grossed out. They are on our skin, and in our mouths, and in our stomachs. They are essential for helping us digest food. Many bacteria are essential for us to be healthy. You can't see them, but you do need them. You are basically a walking zoo! Archaea are similar to bacteria — tiny single cells, about the same size, but with bits and bobs inside that are different enough that we put them in two different domains.

The third domain is eukaryotes. The best way to think of this is that every living thing that is not bacteria or archaea is eukaryotes.

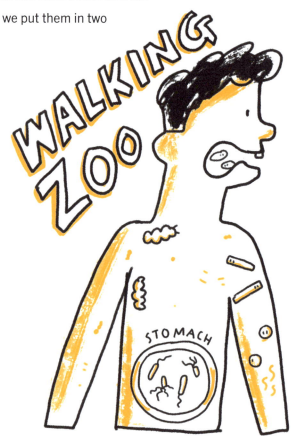

So now we're just dealing with eukaryotes. The next level down is called the **KINGDOM.** Not everyone agrees with this, but the version I like best is that there are five kingdoms within the eukaryotes. Plants belong to one kingdom – including every tree, vegetable, pot plant and weed. Another is fungi (which include mushrooms and funguses that sit on trees, and nasty things like athlete's foot, and yeast that we make bread and beer with, and loads of other organisms). Two other kingdoms are called Protista and Monera – both single-celled and microscopic. But most important for this story is the kingdom of ANIMALS.

Animals include everything that moves, eats and breathes oxygen. We don't really know how many different types of animals there are, but scientists have identified more than 1.5 million so far, and we're discovering new ones every day. Most animals discovered so far are insects – **more than a million different types**. But if you're a blue whale, a wasp or an octopus, or a dog, a crocodile or a duck-billed platypus, or a crab, a spider or a spider monkey, or a penguin, a hamster or a human, you're all in the same kingdom – Animals.

This is admittedly a bit weird as you are probably not very similar to a great white shark or a Komodo dragon (I hope . . .). So we keep going in classifying animals into even smaller groups. The next category down is called **PHYLUM** (FIY-LUM) – which is basically defined by the layout of the animal's body. It might be an arthropod, which has a body in segments and legs with joints, like insects today or trilobites

from millions of years ago. Or a mollusc, which tends to be soft in the middle with a hard shell — like a snail or a clam (octopuses are also molluscs, which is confusing).

Or it might be a chordate, which is an animal with a central spine. A shark or chimp or eagle or bat all have backbones. Spiders, octopuses and slugs do not. All of them are animals, but to get to you, we're interested in things with spines now.

Next comes **CLASS**, and the class we are in is the mammals. Remember, mammals emerged on Earth about the same time as the dinosaurs, and after that massive asteroid landed on Earth about 66 million years ago, the mammals survived, though *we don't really know why*. Maybe it was because they were small. Maybe because they could eat a varied diet. Maybe they could thrive eating all the dead and dying dinosaurs.

The mammals grew bigger and evolved into all sorts of beasts that we know and love today: monkeys, dogs, cows, marmosets, meerkats, gorillas, whales, dolphins, bats, rats and otters, to name just a few. What makes those animals mammals is that they share lots of different characteristics.

Mammals are warm-blooded, which means that we generate our own heat to keep alive, and we don't have to lie in the sun to get warm (although that is a very nice thing to do).

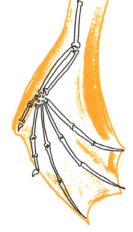

Mammals have hair or fur. You may think, 'Whales are mammals, and they aren't furry', but baby whales and dolphins have hair when they're born – it just falls out as they get older. The main thing which makes those animals mammals is that their mothers feed their babies with milk produced in the mammary glands – which is why they're called mammals.

So far, we've identified about 6,000 different types of mammal (and about 1,200 of them are different types of bats!). Humans may look different to bats or dolphins, but we have many things in common, and these show that we have shared ancestors on the tree of life.

The bones in your hand almost perfectly match the bones in a whale's fin, or a horse's leg, or a bat's wing, but they've evolved to be **stretched** out in different ways depending on whether you're swimming, galloping, flying or playing the piano (or something else humans do).

HUMAN   CAT   WHALE   BAT

Next level down is O for **ORDER** – we, alongside all monkeys and apes, are in the order of primates. Next comes **FAMILY** – the great apes: gorillas, chimpanzees, orangutans, bonobos and us – all similar large apes, but different enough that we can easily tell them apart. Then there's **GENUS**, which are groups of very similar creatures – maybe they've been separated for so long that they look quite different, but they are mostly close enough that they could have babies with each other. We're *Homo* – humans – and there aren't any other types of humans alive these days, so the final classification category is *sapiens*, our **SPECIES**.

HOW TO CLASSIFY YOU

A funny way to remember the order is by a mnemonic. Try this one: ***Dead Kings Play Cards On Furry Gorillas' Stomachs***.

D OMAIN: eukaryotes

K INGDOM: animals

P HYLUM: chordates

C LASS: mammals

O RDER: primates

F AMILY: great apes

G ENUS: *Homo*

S PECIES: *sapiens* <<<YOU

THE SAME BUT DIFFERENT

So if scientists use this system to classify animals, then you can see how us humans might also think it'd be useful to categorise one another too. You might imagine this would be easy because although there are millions of types of animals and thousands of types of mammals, there is only one species of human left — **HOMO SAPIENS**.

Everyone alive today is *Homo sapiens*, but everyone is different. Even identical twins aren't exactly the same (if you know twins in your class, you can probably tell them apart once you've got to know them). We all look different, and we sound different — depending on where we live in the country — and we don't all like the same things.

People also have many ways of describing themselves and putting their identities into categories. That is a form of classification too. Depending on what is being asked, you might answer with details about your: sex, gender, school class, school year, village, town, county, country, sports team, hobbies or job. My youngest daughter is a girl in Year 4 from London who likes drawing, dancing and Taylor Swift. My son is a boy in Year 10 from London who likes football, rugby, PlayStation and Taylor Swift. My eldest daughter is a girl in Year 12 from London who likes movies, books and Taylor Swift.

Categorising is supposed to make things simpler, but humans are complex. So although classification can be helpful, putting things into groups doesn't always tell us everything. It might not seem like this has got anything to do with you, but it all comes back to that question I asked at the beginning, the actual title of this book:

WHERE ARE YOU *REALLY* FROM?

When someone asks you that, they might just be interested or being friendly. But sometimes when certain questions are asked in a certain way, and especially if you have brown or black skin, or look slightly different to the majority, then people might be suggesting that you can't *really* be from wherever you were born (or happen to live). People can assume that you must be from 'somewhere else', maybe somewhere 'foreign', because of how you look.

This is where categorisation becomes unhelpful and narrow-minded. But as we are discovering, the true story of where **EVERYONE** is *really, really* from is much more interesting and reveals how much we actually have in common.

I promise I'll come back to the subject of skin colour and race later — it's very important — but for now the big questions are: how did we end up with only one human species, and how did we get here in the first place?

THE STORY OF HOW WE CAME TO BE

We're going to dive deeper into the story of you and me and how we came to be. I think the story of how humans came to be is the most exciting one in the whole of science. You might like the planets, or fossils, or dinosaurs (**who doesn't love dinosaurs?**), but I like people, and the science of people is always my favourite subject. This is a story of where humans came from, how we moved around the planet, who we met on the way and how the 8 billion of us alive today came to be here. There are a lot of missing pieces in this story, because we've only been

studying it scientifically for about 150 years. During this time, scientists have studied the history of humankind by collecting fossilised bones from around the world and sometimes the tools that our ancestors used thousands, or millions, of years ago: stone axes, spears and even wooden clubs. We've been trying to piece together the story of how we got to be here by looking very carefully at what those old bones looked like and how those people lived, what they ate, what they hunted and so on.

So, nowadays, we can look at old bones and old tools, but we can also look at DNA to work out how one species evolved into another and how humans came to be as we are today. Armed with scientific knowledge learnt from our ancestors and the DNA evidence they've left behind, we can recognise exactly what makes us all human AND what makes us unique.

Our species is called **HOMO SAPIENS**, which kind of means '**clever humans**'— it sounds a bit like showing off, but we ARE the only species to write books or invent PlayStation or aeroplanes, so perhaps it's not a bad name. There have been other species of human, but they didn't invent PlayStation or aeroplanes, and we're the only one left. So in the next chapter we're going to jump from **PREHISTORIC** us to **HISTORIC** us, to find out exactly what happened next and to meet some of your pretty famous human ancestors . . .

CHAPTER 5

ARISE! KING OR QUEEN

We've now worked our way through the birth of the universe and Earth, the birth of life, prehistoric evolution, the primates, the arrival of the hairy humans and then us showing up in Africa around half a million years ago. **Have a breather** and get some water, because this means we are about halfway through the story of where you came from. The first half covered your prehistoric origins, so now it's time to move on to the second part of our story: your historic origins.

We loosely call everything up to the invention of writing prehistory, and everything after that is history. Basically, history begins when we start writing things down. That happened around 6,000 years ago, somewhere in the Middle East.

In fact, the earliest example of a full sentence is from the language of the ancient Canaanites and is engraved into a comb nearly 4,000 years old. The message is short and sweet and says:

May this tusk root out the lice of the hair and the beard

But you know what? We don't even have to go all that far back in history to discover how closely related all humans are.

In 2022, before she died, there were lots of celebrations for Queen Elizabeth II's seventy-year jubilee, making her the second-longest reigning royal in history (Louis XIV of France clocked up seventy-two years on the throne before dying in 1715 of gangrene — the same smelly rotting flesh disease that was in the pus-soaked bandages of the soldiers mentioned in chapter 2).

We love learning about history, and lots of the history we learn in school involves royalty. You might know, for example, that Queen Victoria married her cousin Albert. Or that Henry VIII had six wives and wasn't very nice to any of them (divorced two, beheaded two, one of them died of natural causes and the other one outlived him after he died of being obese, generally incredibly unwell and genuinely **stinky**). Or maybe you know about Edward II, who probably did a lot of important things, but is best remembered for dying in 1327 by having a red-hot poker shoved up his bum (actually, that's probably not true).

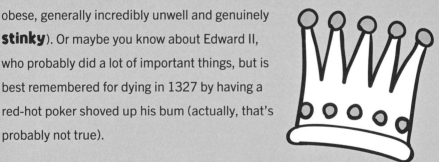

We know the most about these great kings and queens because they are the ones who ruled over the people, which is why they're in the history books. We know the most about them *because* they were royalty, and we don't learn about the lives of most ordinary people in history because they were just normal women and men who had families and worked and did the best they could, but no one wrote books about them, or gave them massive palaces and crowns, or murdered them with hot bum pokers.

People get married, fall in love, have kids, get divorced; they might die, or get remarried, or have kids with other people – families are super complex, and it's never as easy as the family tree on these pages suggests. So in reality, our ancestry tends to be much messier, and family trees aren't neat and tidy. Instead of a family tree with roots, a

trunk and branches, think about a family tree as more like a spider's web. Although 'family web' doesn't have the same nice ring to it, does it? You might think your family is pretty boring too. I'm going to imagine your mum isn't a famous footballer, your dad isn't a TikTok superstar and your sister isn't a princess? Well, it's time to meet some of your ancestors again. Because believe it or not, some of those kings, queens, emperors and warriors — well, THEY are your **ANCESTORS**.

That's right, Your Royal Highness *takes a bow*. To explain why you are personally related to royalty, and perhaps 5,723,642nd in line to the throne, we need to get into the maths, and I promise it'll be worth it.

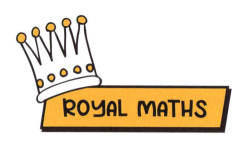

ROYAL MATHS

Some of the maths here is a bit tricky, but don't worry, there won't be a test, only a magnificent discovery at the end, and you should all take a bow, possibly wear a crown and definitely pat yourself on the back for being an extremely excellent human being.

OK, here goes. It starts with something very obvious: *everyone who has ever lived had two parents.*

Whether you know them or not, or live with them or not, every human being is the result of two people: a woman and a man producing a baby. Nowadays, we've invented amazing new technologies which allow women couples to have babies, and other combinations of men and women to start families as they want to, but at the very core of biology, a new baby is the result of a sperm from a man meeting up with an egg from a woman.

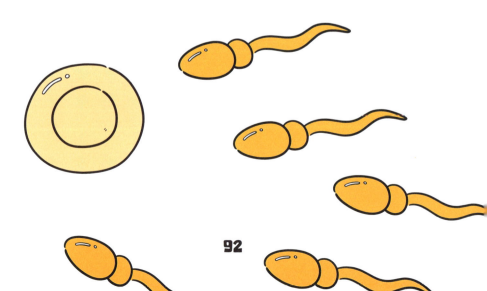

So hang on to this key idea that everyone has to have had two parents. Two parents means that there are two people in the generation directly above you. Now, both your mum and dad also had two parents each – your grandparents – which means you have FOUR ancestors in that generation (you might know some of them, but they tend to be quite old). And you have EIGHT great grandparents, and SIXTEEN great great grandparents, and THIRTY-TWO great great great grandparents, and so on.

We can keep going like this, on and on into the past, but your brain might start to melt and leak out of your ear, and I need your brain to be super powered-up for the next bit. When scientists do these calculations, we make a guess that most people have children when they are in their twenties (even though some people have them younger or older). So we take an average age of about twenty-five to make the sums easier. **That means that every 100 years there are FOUR generations in a family, and you have sixteen great great grandparents who lived a hundred years ago.**

Twelve generations back takes us 300 years into history (12 years x the average age of 25), which means that 300 years ago, you have 2x2x2x2x2x2x2x2x2x2x2x2 ancestors, which works out as 4,096. Which is **LOADS**. You have 4,096 great great great great great great great great great great grandparents. Which would be nice if they all

93

sent you money for Christmas. Unfortunately they've been very dead for a couple of centuries.

But let's keep going back to around 1,000 years ago. What was happening then? The king of England was a dude called Cnut, famous for showing people that despite being super powerful, he wasn't powerful enough to fight against nature and he couldn't stop the tides. The pope was a guy called Benedict VIII, and the archbishop of Canterbury was some fellow called Aethelnoth. This was the time of the birth of  Harold Godwinson too, who became King Harold but got shot in the eye with an arrow at the Battle of Hastings in 1066. High King of Ireland Máel Sechnaill II died, as did Olof Skötkonung, the king of Sweden. The king of Poland was a man called Boleslaw the Brave, which is almost exactly the same spelling as coleslaw. Meanwhile in North Africa, a fourteen year old called Al-Mu'izz ibn Badis took over the government and became the king in Ifriqiya (which is modern Tunisia).

So, roughly 1,000 years ago, there was a lot going on in Europe and the rest of the world. Let's do the maths again for the number of your ancestors.

1,000 years = 40 generations. Which means that the number of ancestors you have is

2x2x2x2x2x2x2x2x2x2x2x2x2x2x2x2x2x2x2x2x2x2x2x2x2x2x2 x2x2x2x2x2x2x2x2x2x2x2x2x2

Which equals . . .

Wait for it . . .

1,099,511,627,776

Let's just spell that out. This would mean that, going back 1,000 years ago, you had **ONE TRILLION, NINETY-NINE BILLION, FIVE HUNDRED AND ELEVEN MILLION, SIX HUNDRED AND TWENTY-SEVEN THOUSAND, SEVEN HUNDRED AND SEVENTY-SIX** ancestors.

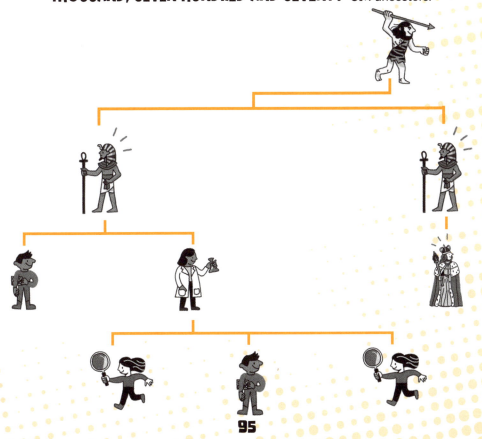

The first time I did this calculation I thought, 'Hold on a minute, this can't be right.' Why? Because when we estimate the total number of people who have **EVER lived**, all the *Homo sapiens* who have been on Earth in the last half a million years, it comes out at about 107 billion. **This is ten times less than the number of ancestors YOU have only 1,000 years ago.**

Erm . . . what is going on here?

Well, it's a little trick, because what it actually means is that there are **1,099,511,627,776 POSITIONS** in your family tree. Which is not the same as the number of individual people. The same person/ancestor can hold many different positions in the family tree.

Real family trees can be messy. It might be that your great great great grandmother had some kids who had some kids who had some kids, and they had some kids who are your 4th cousins – basically complete strangers, who are very distantly related. But if one of them was a man, and another a woman, and they had a baby together, then one of that kid's great great great grandmothers would be their great great great grandmother TWICE. This is actually pretty likely to happen.

Family trees don't keep branching out as you go back through time. They actually begin to collapse in on themselves after a few generations. The lines start crashing into each other, which means that some people are in several positions on your family tree. Can you see now how this explains those massive numbers I came up with?

The further you go back through time, the more the lines collide. One of your ancestors might be your great great great great great grandfather many times over. And as you go back and back through time, something absolutely crazy happens:

All the lines of everyone's family trees crash into each other.

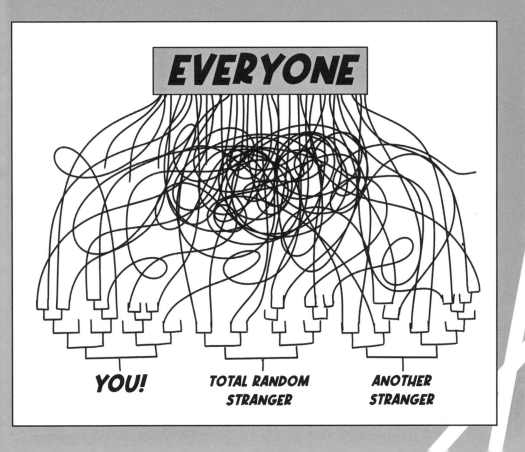

EVERYONE

YOU!   TOTAL RANDOM   ANOTHER
        STRANGER   STRANGER

Now, you might have to take a deep breath before you carry on reading because the maths in this bit gets really wild. When we calculate how deep family trees actually go, we find that a time comes when every single line in your family tree goes through **EVERYONE**. Because all the branches on our family trees cross over at some point in time, it means that the people alive *then* are not just your ancestors, but EVERYONE'S ANCESTORS.

We call it the **IDENTICAL ANCESTORS POINT**. It means that every person alive at that time (who has living descendants today) is the ancestor of *everyone* alive today.

Think about that for a second. Everyone who was alive at the identical ancestors point and has living descendants today is the ancestor of everyone living today.

Working out when the identical ancestors point is requires some even trickier maths, too much to stick on this page (thank goodness!). But when scientists do this calculation for the whole of Europe, the year of the identical ancestors point is:

1,000 years ago.

Remember when we said that you have more than one trillion positions on your family tree 1,000 years ago because all people have two parents? Well, there were only a few million people **ALIVE** in Europe at that time. So every one of those trillion positions has to be filled with someone who was actually alive and that means that, basically, everyone alive is on everyone's family tree at that point in history.

If you were alive in Europe 1,000 years ago, and if you have any living descendants today, then that means that . . .

YOU ARE THE ANCESTOR OF EVERY EUROPEAN PERSON TODAY.

So remember who was alive then: Cnut, Harold, Máel Sechnaill II, Olof Skötkonung, Coleslaw the Brave, all kings in the year 1022. But to know if you are descended from any of those old dead dudes, we would have to know if they have any living descendants today. And we don't know that, because the written records are a bit wobbly. But no problem, let's go back a couple of hundred years, and let me introduce you to Charlemagne.

King Charlemagne was born around the year 742. His name means Charles the Great. His dad was Pepin the Short, King of the Franks (Pepin wasn't actually short, by the way — we're not sure why he had that nickname). The name for the country France, in Europe, comes from the Franks. They were Germanic tribes who travelled from northern Europe into France, which used to be called Gaul.

Charlemagne became one of the great leaders of the Middle Ages. He was king of the Franks, like his dad, then he became king of the Lombards from 774 (which is about half of what is now north Italy). And he became the first Holy Roman Emperor in 800 — basically the boss man for most of Europe. He went on to father at least **eighteen children**.

Lots of people love to look at their family trees and work out who they are related to. And because Charlemagne was a king, we know his family tree really well, and many people today have worked out that he is their x40 grandparent. A family in Holland have traced their family trees all the way back to him. An actor called Christopher Lee (you might know him as Count Dooku in the *Star Wars* films, or as Saruman in *The Lord of the Rings*) also managed to show that his family tree has Charlemagne in it. But Charlemagne was alive before the time of the identical ancestors point. Which means that

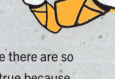

…Charlemagne could be your x40 grandfather too!

You might not be able to show it on a family tree, because there are so many gaps that lead to you from him. But it is definitely true because mathematically it has to be. If Charlemagne has living descendants, and lived before the identical ancestors point, then he is the ancestor of **EVERYONE IN EUROPE**. Which means that if you have European ancestors . . .

YOU ARE A DESCENDENT OF CHARLEMAGNE.

100

Now, this calculation only applies to Europe, by the way, but something similar applies all over the world, we just haven't studied it in as much detail yet. If you're broadly East Asian, **you're almost certain to have GENGHIS KHAN** sitting **atop your family tree.** He was born in northern Mongolia around 1162 and was a famous conqueror who killed thousands, invaded China and had hundreds of children. We are pretty sure that he has living descendants today, which means that he's almost certainly the ancestor of all East Asian people today, just like Charlemagne is for Europeans.

This is an idea that truly scrambles my brain. It doesn't feel like it can be true, but we are very confident that it has to be, and science is all about what we can calculate correctly, regardless of how it feels.

But you are definitely, 100% absolutely mathematically DESCENDED FROM ROYALTY.

It also means you're descended from everyone who came before the identical ancestors point (as long as they have living descendants today). Let's meet some more distant ancestors, shall we? At that time, the Vikings were sailing down from Denmark and Norway and raiding the coasts of

England and France and all around Europe. Some Vikings settled in France and then in 1066 came across to England as part of the Norman conquest.

Well, this means that if you have European ancestors . . .

What's that, I hear you say?

YOUR ANCESTORS WERE ALSO VIKINGS.

And Anglo Saxons, and Romans, and Celts, and fearsome warriors. It also means your ancestors were very normal people from those tribes too: farmers, potters, people who made clothes and shoes, cooks, chieftains, princesses, wise women — basically everyone. This

calculation works for people who have European ancestors. But, for example, many people in the UK today migrated from all around the world, and so don't have any Europeans in their family trees from hundreds of years ago. But don't worry, it doesn't make that much difference.

When we calculate the identical ancestors point for the **WHOLE WORLD**, it comes out at about . . . **5,000 years ago.**

The world was a different place back then. Perhaps you've learnt about some of these things at school. The Stone Age was over, and people began making tools and weapons from bronze – the Bronze Age. Writing and the alphabet were also invented, which allowed us to record history. Which means that everyone on Earth today is descended from everyone on Earth at the time of the pyramids, as long as they have any living descendants. It doesn't matter if your parents or grandparents or great grandparents were from South America or Australia or Russia or China or anywhere in Africa, every single one of you has kings and queens and emperors and warriors in their family trees.

WE ARE ALL DESCENDED FROM ROYALTY

CHAPTER 6

THE SKIN I'M IN

We've discovered that humans are all one species. We learnt that our species comes from Africa. And we've found out that all humans alive today are surprisingly closely related. We've travelled the world, moved and lived everywhere, and had families in all those places. And we are all descended from royalty (and everyone else, if you go back a few thousand years).

We've talked about how we are the same, and how we have the same ancestors, and how we are the same species. But it's also important to recognise something obviously true and very important. **We are all different!**

We can't pretend everyone is exactly the same, because that is obviously not true. We look different to each other; we behave differently and like different things. You might be good at maths, or art, or history, or football, or dance. You might like noodles, or burgers, or curries, or pasta.

Scientists who study humans **(ANTHROPOLOGISTS)** like to try to understand how and why people are different and have different likes and dislikes. Some of these differences are biological, which means that we have different genes. Some differences are social or cultural, meaning that they are things that we learn through living our lives with family and friends and in society and our environment: how we dress,

our hobbies, our opinions. Lots of things are a bit of both: your genes might mean you are naturally quite good at maths or running, but you only really get good at maths or running by practising. It's a bit like having soil rich in nutrients — we still need to plant the seed and tend to the plants.

Some things appear very different between us — the colour of our skin, or the texture of our hair, or the language we speak, or the place where we, our parents or grandparents are from. These things can make us feel very different to other people, especially if those differences are used to insult us or to tell us that we are not as good at some things as other people.

We are animals who are a very complex mix of our genes and our environment and culture. To understand that, we can look to how our history has introduced differences into our bodies, and how our culture has changed our behaviour.

In the earlier chapters, we dealt with the very deep prehistory of humans and our shared family trees in the last couple of thousand years. We've talked about how lots of the history we know comes via rulers — kings, queens and emperors — and these are people who are important in shaping our cultures.

Throughout history, some people have had more power than others. Some rulers have been fair-minded and looked after the people they ruled over; others have been monsters who waged wars and ruled with violence and cruelty. In the last few thousand years, and even more so in the last few hundred years, we travelled more and more around the world and met people who were different to us — exploring and trading, but also fighting wars and conquering nations.

THE STORIES WE TELL OURSELVES

Some people want to rule over others. Maybe they want their wealth, or to control other people, or to spread their own beliefs. Throughout history, the distribution of resources has been unequal — some people became rich when others were poor. Some people had more goods to sell, and others simply seized the possessions of others and violently took over their lands.

For example, the explorer Christopher Columbus discovered the Americas. **Except there were MILLIONS OF PEOPLE living there already, and they didn't need to discover where they lived.** Columbus was the first European to land in the Americas, but we should also remember him for his shocking cruelty and murderous actions in trying to take over the lands he had just found. One of the things Columbus used to do was to cut the hands off

the indigenous people he met and hang them around their necks to warn other people not to cross him. He was an absolute monster.

History is full of people who did incredibly cruel things to others. One of the ways that people in history have justified conquering other nations is by believing that they are somehow *better* than other people. It might be that they think they are cleverer, or more sophisticated, or have more advanced technology, or have the correct religious beliefs.

There are lots of differences between people from around the world, some based in genetics, some based in our lived lives and culture. One of the most obvious ones, the one we see with our eyes as soon as we look at another person, is **PIGMENTATION** — the colour of their skin.

COLOUR CODED

Skin colour is the first thing we might notice when we meet someone new, and it has been used for hundreds of years as a means of ranking people, and for powerful people to believe that they are superior.

Pigmentation has been an indicator of race and the basis of racism for several centuries, and here, we're going to investigate **HOW THAT HAPPENED** and **WHAT IT MEANS**.

As a species, we use all of our senses, but our sight is very strong. Two Labradors are hard for us to tell apart — even their sex (unless we look really closely!). A Labrador would probably have the same problem telling two humans apart, although they may be more likely to smell the difference! **We're not like dogs, who sniff each other's bums when they first meet.** We don't lick people to see what they taste like (that would be super weird, so please don't do that).

GETTING TO KNOW YOU

AND THIS IS PERHAPS COOLIDGE'S BEST-KNOWN PAINTING, DOGS PLAYING POKER

AND HERE WE WE HAVE ONE OF HIS LATER, LESS FAMOUS WORKS – GETTING TO KNOW YOU

Bats rely on their hearing. They use **ECHOLOCATION BY CHIRRUPING** and listening very carefully to where the sound is bouncing around.

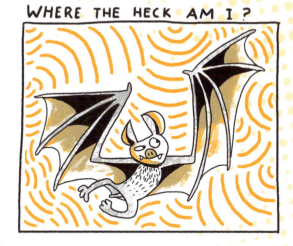

WHERE THE HECK AM I?

But humans establish physical differences between one human being and another immediately, and often the cultural differences too, initially through our sense of sight. One of the most immediately obvious differences is skin colour. Of course, you'll also notice their hairstyle and height and whether they're a boy or a girl, but skin colour is immediately noticeable and covers a bigger surface area than anywhere else. The way our vision works is that we see in three main colours (red, blue and green) and our brains mix them up, so we actually see many different colours.

In relation to people, the words we use to talk about our skin colour are very simplified. We talk about people being Black, or White, or sometimes Brown. But look around your classroom. Does anyone *actually* have white skin, like a piece of paper? Does anyone have black skin, like Darth Vader's helmet? Of course not. Describing skin colour in these ways is not very precise.

In fact, there are **millions of different skin colours,** and they change over your lifetime and on different parts of your body (the soles of your feet or palms of your hands are not the same colour as the skin on your face or arms). And skin colour changes when you spend time in the sun too.

Over a billion people live in Africa today. There are millions of people in Britain with African or Caribbean families. Do you think they all have the same skin colour? They don't, but we call these people Black. Why?

Think about the way we describe eye colour too. Brown, hazel, green, blue. But if you look closely, **there are a range of different eye colours**. The variety can be amazing – from the palest blue to the darkest brown, and everything in between. Some people have flecks of other colours, or rings or sections which are a completely different colour.

EYE COLOUR HETEROCHROMIA

The genes you inherit from your parents have a big role in determining what eye colour you'll have. But it is very complex. In rare cases, some people can have one set of eye colour genes active in one eye, and a different set of genes active in the other eye, meaning that they have two different coloured eyes! This can result in a pattern called heterochromia. Some dogs have this, particularly huskies.

So now that we've talked about how complicated and varied colour is – of eyes and skin – and how White people aren't white and Black people aren't black, you might be wondering, why do we even talk about skin colour in this way?

To get to the bottom of this, we need to do some history. It comes down to the history of science, which is very closely tied to the history of racism. Remember when we talked about classification in an earlier chapter? Well, that's going to become all-important here, so we need to cover this again – because this explains the politics and deeper reasons underpinning racism.

WHEN PEOPLE GET IT REALLY WRONG!

Remember the little phrase to help us classify living things:

Dead Kings Play Cards On Furry Gorillas' Stomachs

The _Gorillas' Stomachs_ is the important bit here. G and S stand for genus and species. Chimps are _Pan troglodytes_. Cats are _Felix catus_. Gorillas are _Gorilla gorilla_ – which admittedly is a bit

DOMAIN: eukaryotes

KINGDOM: animals

PHYLUM: chordates

CLASS: mammals

ORDER: primates

FAMILY: great apes

GENUS: _Homo_

SPECIES: _sapiens_

113

confusing because the species name is the same as the genus name. Sorry about that. And we are *Homo sapiens*.

That is the system that we use today in science. This technique of naming and classifying things is called **TAXONOMY** and was invented in the eighteenth century by a Swedish man called Carl Linnaeus. He wanted to classify all living things – plants and animals –including us, so that we could study them, and name them, and work out the families they belonged to. Linnaeus knew that people from around the world looked different to one another, and he added another category to make the distinction between species.

Later, some scientists tried to name a subspecies of gorilla, and the name they gave to one group of gorillas was *Gorilla gorilla gorilla*. Obviously this is ridiculous, and again, I apologise, but that's the way it is. **What can I say?**

Linnaeus was working at a time when Europeans were exploring the world and taking over many countries in Africa, Asia and the Americas. Europeans were building empires by colonising other countries and, in many cases, enslaving or murdering the people who already lived there.

Linnaeus (and lots of others at this time) looked at the people from around the world and put them into categories based on their appearance. The first thing they used to classify people was skin colour. He invented four categories of human: 1) Africans with 'black' skin, 2) Asians with 'yellow' skin, 3) Native Americans with 'red' skin and 4) Europeans with 'white' skin. He based these on four varieties of human because of the four continents at the time: Europe, America, Asia and Africa. (Now, of course, we know there are seven continents).

Even though this was a long time ago, these labels have somehow stuck, although we can see they're really silly and not at all helpful. Native Americans (that is, people who lived in the Americas *before* Europeans arrived and took over) do not have RED skin, just as people from East Asia don't have YELLOW skin. People from Africa have darker skin on average than most Europeans, but there are more than a billion people in Africa today, and millions more around the world whose recent family came from African countries, and their skin colour varies hugely, and it's certainly not BLACK. But those labels became the basis of categorising humans for centuries to come.

Unfortunately these categories weren't based only on physical characteristics. Linnaeus (and lots of other philosophers, thinkers, politicians and scientists) added other things that he claimed were part of the behaviour of the people he was trying to categorise.

Now, you need to take a deep breath here,

because what they said is deeply racist and comes from a time when many people thought that racism was OK.

Linnaeus and many of the other scientists at that time didn't just classify different types of humans, they also ranked them — as in, from who was best to worst. White Europeans were the best, and all other people were inferior. According to Linnaeus's work, Africans were lazy, Asians were greedy, Native Americans were stubborn, but Europeans were intelligent, worked hard and obeyed the law. We know this is crazy and offensive, but at the time people just believed this. Linnaeus wasn't the only person trying to categorise people, either. All of the attempts to do this had the same thing in common — they were all done by European men, and all of them believed that Europeans were the best, and there was nothing anyone could do about it. We call this 'scientific racism', where people claim 'science' makes these facts true.

IN ACTUAL FACT, IT WASN'T SCIENCE AND IT WASN'T TRUE, BUT IT WAS (AND IS) VERY RACIST.

Obviously nowadays if someone came out and said these awful things, they'd get into a lot of trouble, because they are *scientifically* wrong as well as being cruel and racist. We have to be careful when we talk about people like Linnaeus today. He's an enormously important person in the history of science, and many of the things he did are great and form the basis of how we do science today. But he lived and worked in a time when racism was much more acceptable and most people in Europe truly believed that White people were superior to all others. The early scientists in the eighteenth century thought that skin colour told us how people behaved and even if they were honest or lazy, and that you could tell what a population was like based on their skin and hair. They ranked people based on these colours, and used this to justify taking over their countries and, in many cases, enslaving them.

To our ears today, it's kind of incredible that these 'facts' were widely believed to be true. And unfortunately some of those names, such as white and black, stuck. Yellow was a racist term throughout the twentieth century and thankfully we don't see it much these days. But redskin and Red Indian were used to describe Native Americans until very recently, and the Washington American football team only scrapped the name 'Redskins' — a name it had for 87 years — in July 2020 after years of pressure to do away with it because of its racist connotations against Native Americans.

So when we look at history, we can see that the way we talk about race today comes from a time when racism was considered normal, and names that we continue to use today are often to do with completely ridiculous descriptions of skin colour from hundreds of years ago, and are a really **terrible** way of categorising humans.

LINNAEUS DIDN'T HAVE A CLUE!

CHAPTER 7

WHAT IS THE TRUTH
ABOUT SKIN COLOUR?

People obviously *do* have different skin colours, and people have written about this throughout history. In some of the writings of the ancient Greeks, they would refer to the skin colour of their frends and enemies. Even the name of the African country Ethiopia comes from the Greek words meaning 'darkened face'.

In the paintings on the walls of ancient Egyptian buildings, we can see a range of skin colours. You might think of the ancient Romans and Greeks as being pale-skinned because of the white marble statues that we still have in our museums. **Actually**, scientists have found traces of brightly coloured paints in the cracks of those statues and classical historians think that these statues were painted in a huge range of bright colours. It's just that in the thousands of years since they were made, the paint has **washed off** and just left the white marble beneath.

Today we can look at the genes involved in skin pigmentation. We know already that white skin evolved in response to people moving away from the equator, where the Sun is the hottest, but that isn't the only reason why skin colour varies around the world. If that was the case, then you would simply expect to see skin darkest at the equator and lightest the further you go north. That is very broadly true, but within Africa, we see lighter and darker skin colours up and down the continent. And we see lighter and

120

darker skin colours all over India, and in the Far East, and in Australia.

As always with biology, when we look properly, we see very complex patterns that aren't very easy to understand. But when people first tried to classify humans by skin colour in the days of '**scientific racism**', they simplified to the point of being crazily and obviously wrong.

When we use **DNA** to try to understand skin colour (as well as eye colour and hair colour — all the things that were used to invent the 'races'), what we actually see is that the answers are very, very complex: there are dozens of genes involved in pigmentation, and slight differences in those genes contribute to differences in skin colour. And because we can now get **DNA** out of people who are already very dead, we can try to work out what colour skin people had thousands or even tens of thousands of years ago.

What do we see? Well, we do know that our ancestors tens of thousands of years ago in Africa had darker skin than the White Europeans today, but it was quite varied. In fact, we can tell that African humans who weren't *Homo sapiens* had varied skin pigmentation, **hundreds of thousands of years before *Homo sapiens* even existed**.

CHEDDAR MAN

We also know that dark-skinned people existed all over the world, even in Britain. Ten-thousand years ago, there were humans — *Homo sapiens* — here. One chap that we know quite well is known as **Cheddar Man** (because he was found in the place called Cheddar, not because he was into cheese — which, by the way, was not invented until about 8,000 years ago). In 2015, scientists extracted DNA from Cheddar Man's old bones and they found the versions of genes that he had were most closely associated with darker skin and blue eyes. So Black people have been in Britain for **10,000 YEARS AT LEAST**, and yet again, **Cheddar Man is one of our ancestors!**

By looking at DNA from roughly 8,000-year-old bones, from Sweden and elsewhere in northern Europe, we discovered that people started to **EVOLVE** genes that are most closely associated with pale skin. We think this is because of the balance of two chemicals we need to be healthy: vitamin D and folate.

Vitamin D is essential for building up healthy bones, and the way we make it involves ultraviolet sunlight — getting the sun on your skin helps. But the sun can also cause sunburn, or even cancer. Folate helps babies develop healthily when they are growing inside their mothers. But UV light breaks down folate. So to be healthy, we need a balance of sunlight to make sure we make enough vitamin D but don't break down too much folate.

PRETTY CHEESY!

(Note: There is actually a place called Butts Batch about 7 miles from Cheddar Gorge.)

Dark skin helps protect against the strong **ultraviolet rays** from the sun. As we travel north, the UV rays from the sun are weaker. So, thousands of years ago, people survived longer (and had healthier babies) if their skin was paler. Paler skin meant that they could absorb more UV light to make vitamin D. The evolution of pale skin is at least partially because some people moved away from the hot sun at the equator.

BUT! It's **waaaaay** more complicated than that. People have moved around throughout history and settled in different places. Skin colour reflects that, but there are always other things to consider too.

For example, the Inuit and Yupik are indigenous people from very icy northern America. They kept their dark skin, even though they hardly got any sun at all – that far north in the winter, the Sun comes up after 10 a.m. and sets before 4 p.m., which means it would be dark when you arrive at school and dark by the time you get home. So the people who have lived up there for many centuries have adapted to not having lots of sunlight, and get all the vitamin D they need from eating a diet rich in fish – this is another example of **evolving a local adaptation**.

VARIETY IS THE SPICE OF LIFE

Skin colour varies hugely around the world. On *average* skin colour is darker the nearer your ancestors were to the equator, and pale skin evolved because the sun is dimmer the further north you go. But that doesn't explain the whole picture because humans moved about and had families everywhere, and their genes spread in every direction.

All the same, we can see that there is a scientific reason why skin colour varies, meaning this skin colour classification is, literally, skin deep.

Martin Luther King was an American civil rights leader in the twentieth century. He fought for the rights of African American people and helped them achieve equal rights, which they did not get until 1964. The year before, in one of his most important and famous speeches, Martin Luther King said:

> I have a dream that my four little children will one day live in a nation where they will not be judged by the colour of their skin but by the content of their character.

It's a really beautiful idea, and it reflects how skin colour has been such a big part of racism for so long. Right up until 1964, Black people living in America were not allowed, by law, to go to some places where White people went, or to sit in certain seats on buses. Perhaps you've heard about Rosa Parks? She was an activist in the civil rights movement in America. She became famous after refusing to give up her seat to a White passenger on a bus during the time of racially segregated America in 1955.

The UK wasn't the same as America and didn't have formal racially separated areas and laws, but racism and prejudice still existed, even after the passengers from the *Empire Windrush* ship arrived in 1948 to help rebuild Britain after the war. Back in those days, some Caribbean countries were ruled by the British. Lots of people who lived in the Caribbean had fought in the war, in the British Armed Forces. So when they saw adverts asking for help to rebuild, many of them left their country to come and help out in Britain. Unfortunately there was still plenty of racism.

Things have definitely improved since the 1970s and 1980s, when it was still common for White people to 'black up' as entertainment – where they would paint their faces black and then perform a caricature of Black people. When I was growing up, there was even a popular marmalade which had a racist image of black dolls on jam jars.

Thankfully now there is a lot more awareness of important Black historical figures and the positive impact they have had on our society.

BUT RACISM AND PREJUDICE STILL EXIST.

BLACK LIVES MATTER

You might have noticed more people talking a lot about skin colour recently. In 2020, the Black Lives Matter movement became a big subject in America – and then the rest of the world – mainly due to the tragic death of a Black man called George Floyd who was killed by an American police officer. The awareness and concern spread around the world. Many people became concerned at the way our history has been taught in schools, and they **began to ask questions such as: why are there so few people of colour being celebrated in history books**?

To use Britain, where I live, as an example, we now know that people from Africa with darker skin have been present in Britain since Roman times. Some served as soldiers for the Romans, and others as leaders. In Tudor times, we know that people such as John Blanke were paid musicians in the courts of Henry VII and Henry VIII. And by the time of Georgian Britain in the eighteenth century, there were at least **20,000 Black people** all over the UK.

BLM

BLACK LIVES MATTER

BLACK LIVES MATTER

Most people in Britain today are white skinned, but there are literally millions of us who have recent ancestors from all around the world — places like India and Pakistan, or countries in Africa like Uganda or Ethiopia, or the Caribbean. British people today include a huge range of skin colours, largely because their recent ancestors came from countries where the British Empire was in power. What that meant was that people from those countries became British citizens, and many of them decided that they would move to Britain. I am one of them, and you probably know plenty of kids whose parents or grandparents were born in countries around the world but are now citizens of the country you live in. A phrase that I like to use comes from a British Sri Lankan writer called Ambalavaner Sivanandan, who said:

'WE ARE HERE BECAUSE YOU WERE THERE.'

What he meant was that people came to England from around the world because the British came to their countries and took them over. I'm telling this story about Britain because I am British, but the story is much the same all over the world. Millions of African women and men were taken from their homes and families in West Africa and enslaved in North and South America. Today their descendants are free citizens, and they are Americans because their ancestors were forced to come to those countries. People have moved around the world for thousands of years, but people have been moved around too.

Does skin colour matter? Skin colour says nothing about your abilities or your behaviour. **Whether you are Black, Brown or White**, it tells us nothing about what you're like as a person — whether you like cats or dogs, or are good at maths, sports or dancing. It doesn't say anything about whether you are greedy or kind, intelligent or stubborn. All of these things are completely unrelated to the colour of your skin. Skin colour can say something about our family, our ancestors and our background. It can be an important aspect of our identity and culture. And the vast range of skin colours that decorate humanity do create a tapestry that reflects the complex genetic and historical journey of our species. I think that is pretty special. But it tells another human absolutely nothing about our interests, our abilities or, as Martin Luther King said, 'the content of our character'.

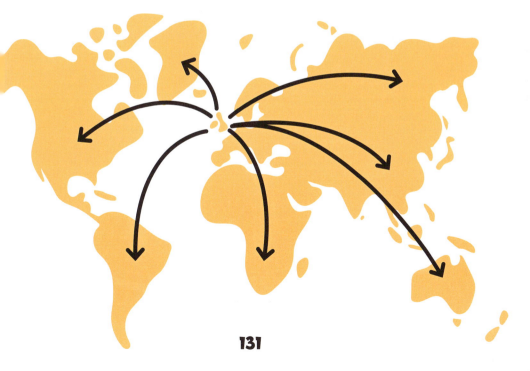

WE STILL HAVE A LONG WAY TO GO

CHAPTER 8

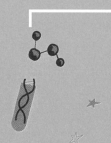

WHAT IS RACE?

Race isn't the colour of your skin. It isn't where you are from. And it isn't even where your family are from.

SO WHAT IS RACE, THEN?

Does it even exist?

Well, the answer is yes. Race does exist because, over the course of time, *we decided that it does.* Back when Linnaeus and the other thinkers and scientists from history thought that race was part of our biology and most obviously linked to our skin colour, they *invented* **racial categories** as a means of describing humans, classifying them and also ranking them.

Many of those scientists also thought that race was a part of your being that could not change. It was fixed in people, and one race of people could not change into another. They thought that qualities of the White race were different from the Black race, and these were locked in the cells in our bodies. This was a time before we even knew of the existence of DNA, but they were thinking along the same lines – that race was a biological part of who you are.

Today, though, we know about DNA and genes and genomes, and we can track the history of our species. We can look at the genes involved in skin colour, and we can see how people migrated around the world in the last few thousand years. And we can compare DNA in people from all over the world. What we have found in the last few years is that DNA is different in everyone, but we also know that you are more likely to have DNA that is similar to your immediate family and neighbours, and to people from the same country.

A geneticist like me can get your DNA out of a sample of your cells if you just spit in a test tube. **But can I just stress that I really don't want to.** The best place for your spit is in your mouth and **pretty much nowhere else**.

With some clever analysis, we can look at the history of where your family has been over many generations. We can see if your mum and dad are from different parts of the world, and if their parents were too. We can see where DNA that is most similar to yours is found in other people on Earth, and from that we can make intelligent guesses about where your ancestors were from.

So does that mean that we can tell what race you are? Absolutely not! Because what we find is that the racial categories that Linnaeus and the other scientists came up with do not match up with what DNA tells us. If you look at people in Africa today, they are all more different to each other than White Europeans are to each other. In fact, if you happen to have Nigerian parents or grandparents, your DNA will probably have more in common with a person from China than someone from Namibia.

When we look at our DNA, what we find is that the way we talk about race doesn't even make sense. How can Black people be a race if Black people are more different to each other than they are to East Asian people?

But not everyone is a geneticist (unfortunately), and we use race as a kind of shorthand for where people are from in the deep past, as it was invented by those old scientists centuries ago, even though what they thought is now known to be wrong.

What that means is that race DOES exist and IS real, but not because it is written in our DNA. Instead, race is what's known as a social construct. This is a kind of technical jargony phrase for things that we all agree on so society can keep on chugging on.

Social constructs are really important too. Do you know what else is a social construct? TIME. Yes, the Earth spins round on its own axis and when it's done a full turn, we call that a day. And sure, when the Earth has done a full loop of the Sun, we call that a year. But why are there twenty-four hours in a day? Why is 12 p.m. lunchtime and 4 p.m. teatime? No particular reason other than we decided that and stuck to it. Without these agreements, everyone would get mad and nothing would get done. Try it at school. Try turning up late for a lesson and then explaining to your teacher that time isn't real, it's just a social construct. Actually, don't try that, because you'll get into trouble. Or if you do, don't blame me.

RUNNING OUT OF TIME

It's the same with money. A one pound coin isn't actually worth one pound at all! It's just we all agree that it has the value of one pound if you exchange it for something. **Money is a social construct in that sense.** But please don't try using this knowledge in a shop. Because they're going to very quickly kick you out the door!

Social constructs work by helping us make sense of the world around us, because they provide order and organisation, much like putting things in categories. So, seeing others with different skin colours and physical features meant that people in our past 'created' the social construct of race, and we still use it today — even though science has pointed out that it's not correct!

INVENTING RACE

We saw in earlier chapters how scientists and politicians in the past decided what the races were, and how we just kind of stuck with it. Those categories were originally invented to show that White people were superior, and therefore they could take over countries and people.

We don't have to feel bad about this now, but it's really important that we know that's what really happened. That way, we can try to prevent it from happening again.

The invention of race was used to justify terrible, truly horrific events throughout history. Evil people have always used whatever they can get

their hands on to justify cruelty, and for much of the last few centuries, racial differences were used to justify slavery, war and genocide – the murder of whole groups of people.

In the eighteenth century, White European people often believed that Black African people were inferior to them, and they used the fake science of race to justify enslaving them. British men were a big part of the business of going to Africa, violently taking people from their homes, locking them in chains and selling them to slave traders. Millions of Africans were enslaved and sold overseas, particularly to the USA and to South America, where they suffered extreme pain, violence and a terrible life as slaves. Scientific racism was part of that. Slave owners believed that Black people were physically strong, but not intelligent. They used scientific racism to justify treating them poorly, not allowing them freedom and preventing them from being educated or free. Similar things happened when the British colonised India and ran the country often with extreme violence and oppression.

The best-known genocide happened during the Second World War, between 1939 and 1945, when Adolf Hitler and the Nazis believed that they were the best race of people (they called themselves the 'master race') and therefore had the right to take over other countries and murder people who they thought were inferior or a threat to their power and purity. The people they hated the most were Jews, and they killed more than 6 million Jewish people during the Second World War. Many died in concentration camps, where the Nazis also experimented on them. But they also persecuted and killed other people too, including Roma people, gay people, people with mental health issues and people with disabilities. Part of their plan was based on the completely false belief that other races were inferior. Every January, there is an International Day of Remembrance to honour and remember those who died.

Today we regard racism as both non-scientific and absolutely hateful. Slavery ended in Britain in the time of Queen Victoria, and over the course of the twentieth century, the country began rejecting its racist history. Britain was part of the forces that fought against the Nazis in the Second World War, recognising that Nazi ideas of White superiority were actually based not on science at all, but on hatred and greed.

Yet it's too easy for us to believe that racism is a thing of the past. There is always room for things to get better, and to continue to fight for a society that treats all individuals with respect and dignity, and looks after them regardless of their race or gender.

But in some countries, fierce wars are still waged on the basis of racial differences. Britain is a tolerant country with laws against being racist in

public and other hate crimes. **BLACK HISTORY MONTH IS CELEBRATED EVERY OCTOBER** and there has been great progress in representing people from around the world in film, TV and sport. Some people have even said to me that Britain is the least racist country they've ever been to! I don't really know how you measure that, and maybe it's true. But it doesn't mean that racism has vanished from my country — the least racist country is still racist, which means we still have work to do. Sadly some negative ideas about race and skin colour having a connection with belonging and ability are still around. For example, there are some people who think a person living in Britain can't be British if their parents weren't born there, or if they have dark skin. In the past, some of these racist ideas were backed by the false science of their day, but there is really no excuse for these beliefs now. This is the same all over the world too, but these prejudices are not true, wherever you are from.

We see racism being expressed all over the world in our culture too. Lots of people get weirdly angry when people with different skin colours appear in films or on TV. You might've seen the recent Disney film *The Little Mermaid*, in which Ariel is played by an extremely talented actor

called Halle Bailey, who is African American. Some people got very cross about this, because in the cartoon version, Ariel has white skin and red hair. They didn't seem to mind that Ariel is a mermaid with a fish tail who can breathe and sing underwater, and Ursula is a weird purple hybrid octopus lady.

I'm sorry to break it to you, kids - mermaids are not real.

But Black people are. So if you know someone who thinks that it's wrong that Ariel is dark skinned, you should probably point out that having a fish tail and having an enemy who is a purple-skinned eight-legged underwater woman is a bit less realistic than having a Black mermaid.

It's crazy to be angry about a Black mermaid, just like it's bonkers to get mad about people not being properly British if they are dark skinned. If you were born in Britain, you're British! But these misguided ideas and the racism that comes with them have been smuggled into the present from the dark days of bad science in the eighteenth century.

This may all feel hard to read and make you feel bad. But I want to reassure you, modern science is no friend to racists. In fact, it is a POWERFUL WEAPON in COMBATING PREJUDICE about people's skin colour and origins.

Let's find out how . . .

JUST KEEP SWIMMING

CHAPTER 9

GO BACK TO WHERE
YOU CAME FROM!

So far, we've discovered that our human story started in Africa, and then 80,000 years ago, a few people started drifting away from Africa. If your mum or dad or teacher thinks you can't sit still, **humans haven't been able to stay in one place for the last million years, so tell them to chill their boots**. Nicely. Maybe our ancestors were following the seasons, or hunting herds, or going where it was good to forage for food. Perhaps food was running out where they lived, so they decided to go off looking for it elsewhere.

You might have moved house before, from one area to another, and it was **PROBABLY** more like that. All this happened very slowly, over many generations — hundreds or thousands of years.

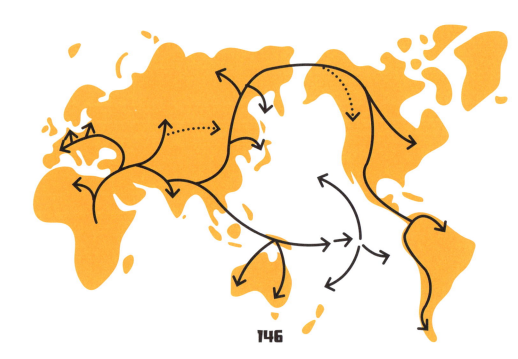

In this chapter, I'm going to show you how understanding this movement, migration and constant coming and going of people has made humans who they are today. **And why it can be used as your weapon for hulk-smashing prejudice.**

Over time, humans spread out from Africa and all over the world. People moved and set up families in every direction.

But actually, it was probably more like this. They moved into Asia, into Europe and down the south coast of Asia, into India and Southeast Asia. Remember that there were no cars, bicycles or planes or ships, so all movement was on foot. When we look at a map of the world today, you might think, 'Well, how did they get there across that huge ocean, if they didn't have boats?'

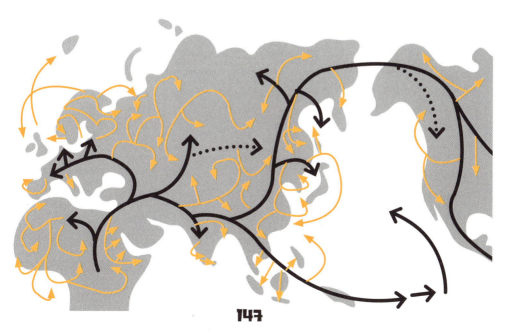

We have to remember that the planet is constantly changing too, and the climate can change the landscape. In the last hundred thousand years or so, there have been multiple ice ages, where the planet has got a bit colder and the ice caps (the North and South Poles) have grown and crept toward the equator. When that happens, sea water gets sucked up into the icy glaciers as they move south (from the North Pole) or north (from the South Pole). Then, the level of the oceans lower and turn what was the seabed into dry land. So, for example, the route from Southeast Asia to Australia wasn't all islands back then: 60,000 years ago, you could walk just about the whole way!

That's how humans first got to Australia – in only 20,000 years we'd gone all the way from Africa to Australia on foot (and probably the occasional paddle boat).

About 20,000 years ago, Asia was also connected to America. Today they are only about 50 miles apart anyway, across the Bering Strait, but back then, it was land all the way too. People had moved across to the east of Asia, what is now northern Russia, and into what is now Alaska without even getting their feet wet. These people were the first people of the Americas. By about 10,000 years ago, the sea levels had risen again, Alaska was cut off from Asia and those founding people spread up and down that huge landmass. They were the ancestors of the Inuit people from the north, Native Americans from the US and Canada, all the way into Central America, where the Aztecs lived, and then into the forests of the Amazon and the very tip of South America too. Over the next few thousand years, the Americas would be filled with people whose ancestors had come across from Asia, long before Christopher Columbus turned up with the intention of forcefully taking over.

In those days, the middle of America was a giant glacier that people wouldn't have been able to get over.

We think they went down to the coast instead. The coast is a good place for people to move to, as it's close to a rich source of food — fish and seafood — so there would have been lots to eat, and it's not a bad place to live.

LET'S GO AROUND!

But Europeans wouldn't set foot in the Americas for thousands of years. And here's another fact for you. Christopher Columbus wasn't actually the first European to land in the Americas. About a thousand years ago, some Vikings, led by a chieftain called Leif Erikson, sailed to what is now Canada. They set up camps in a place called Vinland and stayed there for about three years, where they traded with local people called Skraeling, who they were quite scared of. But there was a big bust-up over a bull that got loose, and the Skraeling were fierce. So the Vikings decided that the best thing to do was to run away. And not come back. Imagine that — big, tough Vikings being scared off by the locals. Maybe the Skraeling had asked the mighty warriors, '*Where are you really from*?'

BRITAIN: A MERRY-GO-ROUND OF PEOPLE

What about Britain? Well, humans have been on the lovely islands of Britain for more than 900,000 years. We're taking Britain as a sort of case study example, because that's where Emma and I were born, but don't worry — I'll move on to explain how this section will still be important to you too, no matter where you're from! Remember that *Homo sapiens* – that is, us – have only been around for about 400,000 years, and only left Africa 80,000 years ago. So we don't really know who these first Britons were – except that they weren't us. We know about them from some amazing footprints of a a a family fossilised in clay off the Norfolk coast, in a place called Happisburgh (actually pronounced: HAZE-BRUH). Unfortunately we do know that these probably aren't your ancestors. They were a species of human that lived in Britain long before *Homo sapiens* left Africa. They weren't the same as us, but based on the footprints we can tell they were another type of human, with size 9 feet. Old bones found in a place called Boxgrove in Sussex reveal they were probably another type of human called *Homo heidelbergensis* (say: HIGH-DEL-BERG-ENSIS), who existed about half a million years ago.

Since then, Britain has had people in it continuously. Although our species probably didn't arrive till around 20,000 years ago, from Europe, we think that Neanderthals were probably here before us.

There were humans – as we'd recognise them today – in Britain 10,000 years ago – people such as Cheddar Man, the darker-skinned, blue-eyed man from the last chapter. These people were mostly hunter-gatherers, meaning that they didn't farm but foraged for berries, vegetables and shellfish, and hunted boar, goats and other larger beasts for their dinner. This period is called the Neolithic, which means 'New Stone Age'. By 6,000 years ago, Neolithic people were all over Britain, making sophisticated stone tools and living in huts, hunting and even beginning to farm.

But then something strange happened. Some people migrated from Europe. We call these people Beaker Folk, early Bronze Age people who are called that because they made bell-shaped clay pots. They turned up and then, fairly quickly, the previous inhabitants of Britain were **GONE**. From DNA found in their old bones, we can tell that in the space of just a couple of centuries, the population was completely replaced! We don't know why or how. It might have been disease or warfare, but the people who were there before basically vanished.

Overnight (well, actually in the space of a century or two), Britain became a Beaker Folk island. It was these European people who built England's most iconic Neolithic monument, Stonehenge. We don't know what they originally intended Stonehenge for, but it was used for centuries by tons of different people to meet, party and pray.

And it still stands today, and on the Summer Solstice in June, all sorts of people come together to meet, party and pray.

The UK has been an island for about 9,000 years. It used to be connected to Europe on the east coast (to the Netherlands), but the sea levels rose and washed away the land off the Suffolk coast in the east of England (where I was born).

Constant changing populations is the true and truly epic story of humankind. For example, Romans, Saxons, Vikings and Normans from Europe were always turning up in Britain, sometimes friendly, other times not so much. One of the ways you can tell how Britain has been such a hub of migration for so long is in the language. English is a completely mad mashup of loads of other languages, which have changed as various visitors arrived, settled, took over or just hung out with the locals.

Here is a perfectly normal sentence:

ON A THURSDAY IN MAY, A WOMBAT PIRATE TOOK A SAUSAGE WITH KETCHUP AND SAILED AWAY ON A DINGHY.

A perfectly normal sentence. Now let's break down that sentence with the origins of those words:

154

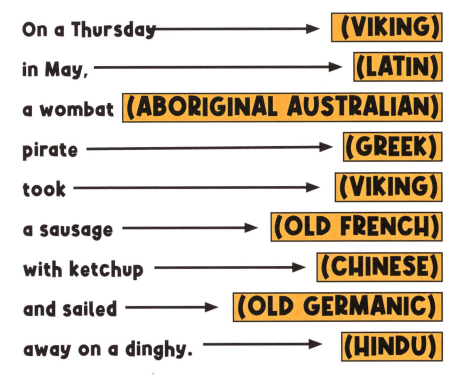

On a Thursday   → **(VIKING)**

in May,   → **(LATIN)**

a wombat   **(ABORIGINAL AUSTRALIAN)**

pirate   → **(GREEK)**

took   → **(VIKING)**

a sausage   → **(OLD FRENCH)**

with ketchup   → **(CHINESE)**

and sailed   → **(OLD GERMANIC)**

away on a dinghy.   → **(HINDU)**

The crazy history of people moving in and out of Great Britain is right there, in the way British people speak.

This constant movement of people is the story of all countries, by the way. Britain is not unusual in being a merry-go-round of people. I've mentioned Australia and the Americas, and Russia and a few other places, but human beings are always on the move. Even within the huge continent of Africa, which has been populated by our species for the very longest time – continuously for maybe half a million years – the movement of people within Africa has also been constant. It might feel like we are stable for years, living in the same place, or even the same house. But over longer periods of time, people have been on the move, trying to survive, and start families, wherever they can.

People move around for all sorts of reasons. One of the reasons is that in modern history, Europeans started seriously exploring the world and often conquering countries with force. The British, and other European nations, began building empires where they ruled over other countries. Eventually it meant that people from those countries that Britain had conquered sometimes came to Britain and had families here. Remember that phrase I used earlier in this book: *we are here because you were there.* Europeans travelled to America and invaded in 1492, almost completely wiping out the Native Americans who were already there. In the nineteenth century, millions of people migrated to the USA to start new lives for their families.

Because of the history of Empire, in the last century, many Black and Brown people have emigrated to Britain, and so they are much more common now than before in UK history. But the truth is that these lovely islands where I was born have always had a constant trail of people coming and going, migrating and leaving, invading and settling, and this is what makes Britain great. That's why the question 'Where are you really from?' makes no sense at all! We are a nation of immigrants whose culture is borrowed from people from all over the world. And there's no better way of showing this than at lunchtime . . .

FOOD, GLORIOUS FOOD!

So let's talk about food, partly because I LOVE food, and I LOVE
cooking, but mostly because I LOVE eating. But it's also a really
interesting way to see how much people move around the world and
share their cultures, often without us realising it.

Sometimes people feel proud of the histories of their countries, and other
times people feel shame. I don't really feel either much – I love it when
our football team wins, like in 2022 in the European Championship, but
when it comes to history, it was stuff that happened and had nothing to
do with me! But that doesn't mean I'm not interested in the past. It's the
opposite way round, in fact – I want to understand the past more so
we can learn from history and try not to repeat the mistakes that
people made.

I also think that humankind's strength is in our diversity. I want
to learn from other people's cultures, and to find out what they are
like and what they like doing. Food is a good way to do this. People eat
different food all around the world. This is partly because, from country
to country, it depends on what is available to farm and hunt in those
places. Some plants grow better in hot climates, some in wet
climates and some in dry. Cultural and religious
beliefs also influence what food is eaten in

157

different parts of the world — for example, most Muslims don't eat beef or lamb if it has not been slaughtered by the halal method, and Jewish people tend to only eat foods that are kosher. And some food and cooking is just tradition — things that are passed down in families and in cultures.

RELIGIOUS BELIEFS ABOUT NOT EATING CERTAIN FOOD

Jewish: Only eat kosher meat and fish. Kosher means that the allowed foods have been selected and prepared in a certain way that fits in with the rules of the Jewish religion.

Muslim: Only eat halal meat and fish. Halal means the animals have been killed in the way that fits with their religious laws.

Buddhist: Many are vegetarian. One of their teachings forbids taking the life of another, and so some Buddhists believe that this means not eating meat.

Hindu: Many are vegetarian, and almost all don't eat beef, as they consider the cow a holy animal.

Many other religions are vegetarian or vegan.

The role that food plays in different cultures and religious beliefs is complicated and varies a lot between individuals and their communities, but it's interesting to discover the differences among us all. And these days, of course, we can get food from all over the world, wherever we live.

One of the most popular meals in the UK these days is chicken tikka. That's an Indian dish, but we think that it was actually invented in England (or maybe Scotland) by Indians in the 1940s, to suit the tastes of White British people who weren't so used to spicy food in the twentieth century – so it's really a British Indian dish. I like my curries spicy, with lots of chilli. But did you know that chillies actually came from South America, and were taken to India in the sixteenth century?

What about heading to the beach for a holiday and sitting down with some delicious fish and chips? Isn't that the most British thing to do on a summer's day? Well, fish and chips was actually invented by Jewish people from Spain and Portugal in the nineteenth century. The potatoes used to make chips are from South America and were only brought to Britain during the sixteenth century. And ketchup (a Chinese word) is made from tomatoes, which are also from South America. Tomatoes, potatoes and chillies had never grown in Britain until they were brought there from South America. Pizzas might seem very Italian, but in fact flat breads with toppings were being eaten in ancient Egypt thousands of years before the invention of the Margherita.

Or what about a traditional British Christmas dinner? Well, that's almost as international as you can imagine: turkeys originated in Mexico. Potatoes, South America. Carrots and peas? They originated in the Middle East.

What about fruit? Surely there's nothing like a juicy British apple? Actually, apples originated in Asia. Watermelon in West Africa, grapes in the Middle East, mango in India, tangerines in East Asia, and pineapples, blackberries, blueberries and cranberries are all from South America.

One of my favourite foods is sushi, which is from Japan. I like rice rolls stuffed with cucumber (which originated in India) and avocado (which originated in South America) and prawns (which swim around in the oceans all over the world).

What we eat is truly international. What's your favourite food? Whatever it is, it's probably made up of ingredients from all over the world. So, much like humans, food has migrated around the world, planted roots in places it didn't initially come from and become a crucial part of the culture, identity and land of those places.

GO BACK TO WHERE YOU CAME FROM!

No one is born a racist. Within a few days of being born, babies can see that one person looks different from another. This means that they can recognise their parents. They can also tell the difference between colours, even if they can't name them yet. This includes different skin colours, of course. But these differences have little meaning for a baby. There is no judgement attached to them, positive or negative.

People who are racist have learnt to be that way. It may be that they have been taught to be suspicious or even hate people who look different to them, or to believe that somehow other races are inferior to them. The reasons for this have a long and complicated history, as we saw earlier on.

The title of this book, the question

WHERE ARE YOU REALLY FROM?

is something that often gets asked, and sometimes it might mean:

'WHY DO YOU LOOK DIFFERENT TO ME?'

You might have even asked someone the question yourself. Maybe you were just interested in why someone looked different. But it's often been a question that is loaded with judgement. Many mixed-race or ethnic-minority people get asked this question, and while it's mostly well meaning, sometimes it can be really pointed, as if to say,

'YOU'RE NOT FROM HERE,'

or even

'WHY ARE YOU HERE?'

Sometimes — thankfully not very often these days — it might be phrased as a straight-up insult:

'GO BACK TO WHERE YOU CAME FROM!'

Racism like this is a form of bullying, and I don't like bullies. Britain, where I was born, has been home to travellers and immigrants throughout history. The only true indigenous Brits occupied the land almost one million years ago and we're not even sure what *species* they were! Because I know about the history of humankind, and how we've migrated all over the world, when somebody says, 'Go back to where you came from,' I don't really have any idea what they mean, only that they *are* mean.

These are hurtful things to say, and they are meant to make people feel unwelcome and that they don't belong here. But they are also silly things to say, and although it isn't easy to stand up to others, it's important to make the bullies who say this look silly and to take their power away.

So if someone ever says to you or your friends, 'Where are you *really* from?' or 'Go back to where you came from!' you can laugh at them and ask them what — *or when* — do they really mean?

This morning? Or a thousand years ago?
Your town, street or house? Where you were born?
Humans are all from Africa originally.
I'm a human being, and I'm from Earth, same as you.

HOME SWEET HOME

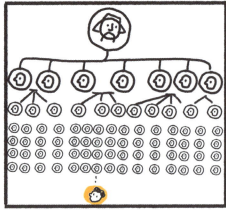

CHAPTER 10

MYTH BUSTING

When we first meet someone, we quickly form ideas about them. It's a very natural, human thing to do. We make assumptions about people as soon as we see them. These assumptions are called stereotypes.

STEREOTYPES AND PREJUDICE

Have you ever heard the phrase **'Never judge a book by its cover'**? Basically, this means that we shouldn't make assumptions about someone or something until we have investigated and understood them better. (However, you should judge this book by its cover, because the cover is awesome.)

Equally, you might say, **'Never judge a human by their colour.'** This is another way of referring to stereotyping.

Stereotypes are beliefs we might have about what a person or a group of people are like. Stereotypes can sometimes be helpful to understand the world, as long as we remember that stereotypes are often untrue, and some stereotypes are deliberately harmful. Grouping together individuals and forming an idea about them, without knowing them personally, is an example of a stereotype. People form all sorts of stereotypes based on race, gender and class.

Maybe you know what this feels like. Have you ever had someone judge you? Perhaps it was based on where you're from, how you look or speak, the things you like doing or the clothes that you wear? If you have, then you'll know it's not very nice.

If we make assumptions about someone based on just their gender, beliefs, appearance, religion or race, it can not only be disrespectful, but also very hurtful. Even though we shouldn't judge a book by its cover, it does happen. Many of us have built-in prejudices that we may not even be fully aware of. Prejudice means we have a negative idea about certain people. It literally means *pre-judging* – deciding what someone is like before you've actually found out for yourself. But when we use stereotypes, we stop seeing the real person, the unique individual, and that can become dangerous.

Ask yourself these questions:

Who cries more often - boys or girls?

Who is better at football - boys or girls?

Who is best at cooking - boys or girls?

Who is best at video games - boys or girls?

I bet you had some ideas about the answers here, didn't you?

But in truth, there are no right answers. These questions highlight stereotypes about gender that are harmful. Stereotypes like these can have the effect of telling people what they should or shouldn't do, no matter whether they are any good at them or not. A stereotype could even stop them from trying an activity they'd enjoy, or from expressing themselves.

Emma finds it irritating when people are surprised that she loves sci-fi movies and hates shopping — which she's supposed to like, *being a girl.*

I cry at movies all the time, even when they're not sad. I cried when Rey got the lightsabre in *The Force Awakens*, and in *Wonder Woman* when Diana came out of the trenches in the First World War. Who is better at football? Well, some people would assume that the men's England football team would perform better in international competitions, but it was the women's team that won the **European Championships in 2022**, whilst the men have never won. So who is better?

There can also be stereotypes about geography, ethnicity and religion. Stereotypes can be negative or positive. Some stereotypes *sound* positive: Black people have 'good rhythm' and make great athletes or dancers, or people from East Asia are good at maths, or people who wear glasses are clever – but it's important that you understand these ideas can also be harmful.

Maybe you've experienced being stereotyped, or someone you know has?

Stereotypes can be bad because they can stop us looking at the whole person. If we believe stereotypes, they stop us getting to know the new person who has joined our class or moved into the area. We could be missing out on meeting a future friend, or we could be signalling to someone that they shouldn't do something they love or they should do something they don't enjoy. And, if we aren't careful, stereotypes can easily become prejudices.

To stop us falling into the trap of using stereotypes, we should ask ourselves a few questions about those stereotypes.

Are they true?

Are they hurtful to the person?

Where does the stereotype come from?

If they are true, is it because they were born that way or have learnt to be like that?

Of course, these are very hard questions to answer, and they require proper work. We need to know why those stereotypes exist, which means studying history. We need to know how people feel about them. And we need to try to unpick what is in our DNA, and what is stuff that we have learnt. Who we are is a mix of our genes and our environment, and believe me, it's incredibly hard to pick them apart – that's the work of some of the most brilliant scientists working today, and they still don't even really know!

We inherit our genes from our parents, but we also learn behaviours from our families too. This is sometimes referred to as **NATURE** and **NURTURE**: nature is your DNA; nurture is the environment in which you live and were brought up – basically everything that is not DNA!

Our culture plays an important part in who we are too. Maybe you're into Bollywood movies because you have Indian family. Or maybe you've never tasted meat because your family are vegetarian.

Or consider the language that you speak. Physically being *able* to speak is something that is encoded into our DNA. It's genetic, meaning that we have genes which give us the ability to say words and construct sentences, and to communicate complex ideas from a very young age. But the actual *language* you speak is determined by the country and family you're born into. I speak English because I was born in England to English parents. If I'd been born in Spain to spanish parents, I expect **yo hablaria español**!

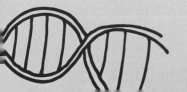

Many stereotypes are based around sport. Maybe you love football, tennis or gymnastics. Even if you're not interested in sport, it's a big part of our lives around the world, and so you've probably at least heard of Venus Williams or Marcus Rashford.

More people on Earth watch the Olympic Games than any other event on TV. Sport is one way that people from all over the world perform at the peak of their physical capabilities. And it's great entertainment. We compete in sports partly for the fun of the game, but also to win, and that means we see that some people are better than others at certain sports and some countries do better than others. But often racial stereotypes emerge from seeing elite sportspeople in action.

Let's look at stereotypes associated with race and see if we can answer some of those earlier questions.

There is a popular idea that Black people are in general better at sport. The first question we should ask is this: is it true? We'll look at some numbers — and at a glance you might well think it is true:

- **There hasn't been a White sprinter in the Olympic 100 metres final since 1980**

- **All of the major long-distance records since 2010, and every winner (men and women) of the London Marathon since then, has been either Kenyan or Ethiopian**

- **40% of footballers in the top four leagues are Black – and in the UK only 3% of people are Black**

So, at a glance, it looks like more Black people do play sport at a higher level. BUT:

- **In 2019, 73,000 competitive swimmers were registered with Swim England but only 668 – less than 1% – identified as Black or mixed race**

- **In the Olympic swimming finals, there have only been two Black swimmers in its entire history**

- **In 2020, on the cycling World Tour, there were only 5 Black cyclists out of 743, and 1 out of 143 in the Tour de France**

So what is happening here? If Black people are so naturally athletic, why are they almost entirely absent in some sports? It's clear that in some sports, Black people are over-represented and yet in others they are under-represented.

In sport, different body types, and different metabolisms, do make a huge difference to success. An obvious example is that tall people tend to be better at basketball.

Height can be quite an advantage in sprinting too: Usain Bolt is 6 ft 5, one of the tallest sprinters of all time. His height is part of his success as the fastest man in history. The speed at which he can take a step is about the same as the other sprinters he beats, but because he's taller, his stride is a few inches longer, so he takes fewer steps to finish 100 metres.

Being good at long-distance running is very different from being good at sprinting short distances. People who are good at one aren't necessarily good at the other.

This is partly because there are two different types of muscle cells – fast and slow twitch – and they have an effect on how naturally you can perform either sports that need explosive energy or endurance sports such as long-distance running. People who are good at long-distance running have more slow twitch muscle cells, which are better at processing oxygen to generate the energy to move. Fast twitch cells are better for producing explosive energy over a shorter time. People who

173

are good at sports that require explosive energy tend to have a higher proportion of fast twitch muscle cells.

On average, people from East Africa tend to have more slow twitch cells too. This is because their ancestors lived at a high altitude where there is less oxygen, so they have evolved to have a more efficient way of processing it. This gives them an advantage when competing at sea level with people who don't have the same physiology, because there is more oxygen at sea level.

These things help give people from these areas and countries a distinct biological advantage in long-distance running, **but it only PARTLY explains their success**.

This shows that there *is* a genetic factor to sporting success, but that isn't the only reason. These advantages aren't limited to one race or group of people. The long-distance runners from East Africa are very different from the most successful sprinters from America, even though they are both Black. When you look more closely, the argument is beginning to fall apart. Maybe your grandparents were from East Africa, but you're terrible at running or just don't like it at all (I can't run more than 200 m without getting knackered, but I am quite good at sprinting — at least I used to be before I got all creaky and old).

If long-distance runners are all from East Africa, then why aren't there more Kenyan endurance cyclists? That's a sport that needs slow twitch muscle cells and incredible abilities to process oxygen. The Dutch are the tallest nation, and yet they're not known for being amazing at basketball. India has 1.2 billion people and a fantastic cricket team, but can you name me a famous Indian footballer? There are more than a billion Chinese people, but as a nation they're not very good at rugby. Is that because there is something special about Chinese people, or is it that rugby isn't popular in China? **What do you reckon?**

Some people have suggested that African Americans who are descended from enslaved people have gained an advantage in physical activity, including sport, as a result of being enslaved. But this doesn't make any sense. Examining the genetics of African Americans, there's no evidence for this at all.

Remember, to be excellent at sport takes a certain mindset — of dedication, practice and extremely hard training. Most of us who enjoy sport want to do our best, and to be a **Lionel Messi, Venus Williams** or **Lewis Hamilton**, you need a special combination of raw talent, a particular physique, training and access to training facilities and coaches.

That last bit is really important and explains why we can see such differences in countries' successes in different sports. African countries are yet to produce a world-class skier. Can you guess why?

Countries with no coasts don't tend to produce very good sailors. Swimming is a great example of how the sports you play, and get good at, can be defined by where you live and your culture. Despite huge successes in

certain sports, Black people (Black British, African American or from Africa) are nearly completely absent from top-level swimming competitions.

In the past, many people have suggested that there is a genetic reason for this, which is that Black people have denser bones and therefore don't float as well as White people. **If you're thinking that sounds stupid – you're right, it is!** It's a ridiculous and racist argument which is not true at all. There is no difference in bone density between Black and White people, and even if there was, it wouldn't make much difference to how well you float. This is a classic example of scientific racism – trying to find a biological reason to explain why one race of people is inferior to another.

But it is true that in America, many Black people can't swim (around 60% don't swim, but 60% of White Americans do). **So why is this?**

Now, this is going to sound very silly, but the main reason is that *you need to be taught how to swim*. No one can swim without being taught because we are not dolphins. When the reasons for why there are so few Black swimmers was studied in America, they found that swimming pools are usually built in areas where few Black people live, and that if parents don't swim, they tend not to teach their kids, and that swimming lessons cost money and time. All of those things relate to *actually being taught how to swim*, and not some magical made-up sinking factor in your bones.

Another reason is role models. People get into hobbies and jobs because they see people who inspire them. I became a biologist because I love **David Attenborough**. Sport is just the same, and many kids take up sports and want to be like their heroes and heroines — it might be their moves you're copying on the gymnastics team or football field. But if you don't see any people who look like you doing a certain sport, then you're less likely to take up that sport in the first place.

For example, my co-author Emma used to sprint at school, but the only role model runner she remembers being around at that time was **Zola Budd** (a South African long-distance runner back in the eighties, who was famous for running in bare feet). Zola Budd and Em didn't have much else in common — though Emma did used to run without shoes on to be like her hero!

People from around the world excel in different sports, and although there's definitely a physical element, being good at sport is also highly determined by your culture, access to training, role models and the popularity of that sport in your country or region.

It is good to be aware of stereotypes and where they come from because then we can be more aware of not using them. You might think being sporty is a good thing. Who doesn't want to be faster, or stronger, or more muscly? Isn't it a positive to say that a certain group of people are good at a certain sport?

That's where the history comes in. In the days of Empire and colonies, the people who invented the racial categories — remember Carl Linnaeus from our earlier chapter? — decided that White people had superior brains and that Black people were physically strong but less intelligent. We know that this is definitely not true today, but it was used as justification for enslaving them.

So you can see that this idea of Black people being better at sport is rooted in the history of scientific racism. It's such a common idea in our society that we don't even notice it. A big study of sports commentators in America showed that when they were talking about Black athletes, they often spoke about their bodies and strength, but when they talked about White athletes, they talked about their hard work and intelligence. This is yet another example of scientific racism.

When it comes to sport and race being linked, it might seem like certain groups of people from certain countries are better than others. But when we look closely, we understand that success isn't because of someone's race, but a complex mixture of biology, psychology, culture and environment.

Sport is one of the most **exciting**, **fun**, **dramatic** celebrations of what humans can do when they put their mind to it, train and work hard. Natural talent is real, and our bodies can determine what sports we excel in. The best gymnast on Earth right now is a young African

American woman called **Simone Biles**. She's the best because of what she does — in her own words:

'PRACTICE, PRACTICE, PRACTICE'

AIM HIGH!

FINAL WORD

This is the end of this book. But it's not the end of the story at all, because it's your story. **YOU** are part of the greatest story ever told. An epic 4-billion-year tale of life on Earth, and you carry the story of every single one of your ancestors. It's locked in the genes in your cells, but now we can look at that DNA and tell these stories. You are a walking history book!

The best thing about science and history is that it's never-ending.

We're constantly asking new questions and finding out new things, discovering new old bones and uncovering bits of DNA that we didn't know about, finding new relatives from all over the world and learning about other people's cultures, traditions and histories.

We haven't just learnt about evolution and the story of life on Earth; we've also learnt about how the history of science has been part of some of the worst acts of history. Opinions and prejudices about where a person is from, and the stereotypes spread by these prejudices, continue to create inequality and injustices that make our society weaker, unless we all educate ourselves with **FACTS**!

> **I THINK THE SMARTEST PEOPLE ARE NOT THE ONES WHO KNOW THE MOST, BUT THE ONES WHO ASK INTERESTING QUESTIONS.**

Science isn't just about knowing stuff. It's about finding stuff out. So we're going to need you to get involved. We need you to find out new things so the story continues. Some of the things I've told you in this book have been known for years. Other things were only discovered this year. Next year there'll be more discoveries which will change the story again, and then one day, maybe you will become a scientist and you will correct me! Or maybe you will become a writer like Emma or an illustrator like Adam M, but whatever you do, remember that the best thing you can say when you're asked a new question is, **'I don't know. But I will try to find out.'**

The world is a tricky place. It's completely beautiful and amazing, filled with brilliant people and amazing nature.

But we've also got a whole load of problems to deal with. Racism is part of that, but now we know that science is no friend to racists. We can dismantle sterotypes and prejudices with knowledge about where they come from, and we can wreck hurtful ideas about race with the knowledge of what science actually says.

Not gonna lie — we've got other problems to deal with too. There's global warming and the climate crisis, and the extinction of animals and plants, and poverty and diseases. These are the big issues for us all, because they affect everyone. But if we do more science and more history, work hard and think creatively, then we *can* fix these problems. We can invent new technologies, tell new stories, draw new pictures and have a better understanding of where we come from: not just our own families, but a global history, and as members of humankind.

This way we can make the world a better place for the next generation. That's you. And then it's your children, if you have any. And then it's their children, and on and on into the future. We've been on a crazy, epic journey in this book — billions of years, millions of miles, thousands of generations — to discover where you are really from. But the next question is even more important:

'WHERE ARE WE GOING NEXT?'

GLOSSARY

Accretion: Gradual process of growth, particularly of planets.

Adaptation: How living things change to help them survive or reproduce more successfully.

Ammonites: A group of extinct creatures with spiral shells, which lived in the sea millions of years ago.

Arthropods: Animals with hard shells on the outside and no bones inside their bodies.

Big bang: A scienticfic theory that explains how matter got made, including the stars, the planets — and basically everything.

Bipeds: Animals who walk on two feet.

Carnivores: Animals who eat other animals.

Cell: The smallest unit of animal or plant life.

Chromosomes: Long strands of DNA which contain genes.

Class: One of the ranks of classification in biology. It's above order and below phylum. We are in the class called mammals.

Classification: The way we arrange animals and plants into groups based on their similarities.

Cretaceous: The time from 145 million years ago to 66 million years ago, which is when the humongous meteorite landed on Earth and the dinosaurs went bye bye.

Denisovans: Extinct humans who lived in what is now Siberia in Russia and East Asia.

Domain: The highest order of life classification.

Double helix: The shape of the molecule of DNA — imagine a ladder, and then twist it round like a corkscrew.

DNA (deoxyribonucleic acid): A molecule that makes chromosomes, and is what genes are made of.

Echolocation: When animals (including dolphins, bats and a few others) use sound to 'see' objects.

Evolution: The process of how living things change over time.

Family: One of the ranks of classification in biology. It's above genus but below order. In this system, the family we are in is called hominid.

Genes: Sections of DNA that code proteins.

Genocide: The act of killing an entire group of people, such as a nation or race.

Genome: The total amount of DNA in your cells.

Genus: One of the ranks of classification in biology. It's above species, so we are in the genus called Homo, and although there were lots of humans in this genus in the past (*Homo neanderthalensis*, *Homo erectus* etc), *Homo sapiens* is the only one left.

Great apes: This is another way of describing the family hominids, and contains all the living great apes which are chimps, orangutans, gorillas, bonobos and you.

Habitual bipeds: Creatures who walk on two feet most of the time — us (as adults!), ostriches, kangaroos and more, but not chimps, who can walk on two legs but mostly don't.

Hadean: The name we give to the first geological era on Earth, lasting from its formation 4.5 billion years ago until about 4 billion years ago. Named after Hades, the Greek god of hell.

Herbivores: Animals who eat plants.

Homo floresiensis: An extinct species of human discovered on the island of Flores in Indonesia. They were little people with big feet, so immediately were given the nickname 'hobbits'.

Homo sapiens: The last living species of human, that is, us!

Homo erectus: An extinct type of human that existed from about 2 million years ago and lasted until about 100,000 years ago. We don't think they were our ancestors.

Identical ancestors point (IAP): The time in the past when all family trees smush into each other, which means that if you were alive at the IAP, and have living descendants today, then you are the ancestor of everyone today. For Europeans, that time was about 1000 years ago. For everyone on Earth the IAP was about 4–5,000 years ago.

Insectivores: Animals who eat insects.

Jurassic: The time from 201 million years ago until 145 million years ago. This was the time when the dinosaurs flourished, but also when the mammals came about too.

Local adaptation: Adaptations are the characteristics that organisms evolve to suit their environment. Local adaptations are ones that have evolved because of the place where they live. Polar bears are white because they live in the snow. Inuit people have evolved eating a lot of fish in their diets, and their bodies are adapted to process that food more efficiently than people whose ancestors never ate any fish.

Membrane: A thin layer of fatty molecules that forms the outside of a cell.

Mesozoic: The time (from 252 million years ago till 66 million years ago) when the Earth split from being one giant landmass surrounded by sea into separate areas — this time was dominated by dinosaurs.

Metabolism: Chemical reactions which occur and change food into energy.

Multicellular: Made up of many cells.

Neanderthal: Early humans who looked like us but had even bigger heads and broad chests.

Nurture: The environment in which you live and were brought up, as opposed to nature, which is your DNA.

Organism: Any living biological thing.

Ovivores: Animals who eat the eggs of other animals.

Phylum: One of the ranks of classification in biology, above class but below kingdom. We are in the phylum called chordate, which is (very broadly) animals with something like a spine or column if they are not very bony.

Pigmentation: Colour, in this case the colour of skin or hair or eyes.

Prehistoric: The time before written records existed.

Primates: Members of the group of mammals which includes monkeys, apes and us.

Species: Related living things which are able to breed together.

Taxonomy: The science of naming and describing organisms.

Tiktaalik: An extinct fishy type thing that lived about 375 million years ago, and was about the size of a sausage dog, which could breathe air as well as breathe underwater.

Triassic: The time from 252 million years ago until 201 million years ago. Reptiles and loads of fish evolved in this time, but there was a huge extinction about 201 million years ago, probably a result of huge volcanoes going off, and more than 90% of all species died.

Trilobites: Marine arthropods from the sea that lived between 521 and 250 million years ago — we have found more than 20,000 different species.

Tsunami: A gigantic wave caused by earthquakes under the sea or giant meteorites crashing into the sea.

ACKNOWLEDGEMENTS

Adam Rutherford

This book is a team effort. It turns out that writing books for children is ever so much more difficult than writing for grown-ups. I owe endless gratitude to my co-authors, Emma, for beating the words into shape, and Adam, for making the pictures zing. As ever, my literary agent and friend Will Francis stands as my partner, though it is never clear which one of us is Han Solo and which is Chewbacca. My biggest, and most humble apologetic, thanks go to the editorial team at Wren & Rook, Helen and Laura, who have tolerated me missing every single deadline they set and I agreed to with grace, and gently pushed me to stop pratting about and deliver the book you are now holding.

Em Norry

Thank you, Ed, for all the laughs, insights and encouragement. This book wouldn't exist without you! And thanks to the two Adams for their brilliance and to the amazing team at Wren & Rook.